An Analysis of

Pankaj Ghemawat's

Distance Still Matters: The Hard Reality of Global Expansion

Alessandro Giudici
with
Marianna Rolbina

Published by Macat International Ltd
24:13 Coda Centre, 189 Munster Road, London SW6 6AW.

Distributed exclusively by Routledge
2 Park Square, Milton Park, Abingdon, Oxon OX14 4RN
711 Third Avenue, New York, NY 10017, USA

Routledge is an imprint of the Taylor & Francis Group, an informa business

Printed by CPI Group (UK) Ltd, Croydon CRO 4YY

www.macat.com
info@macat.com

Cataloguing in Publication Data
A catalogue record for this book is available from the British Library.
Library of Congress Cataloguing-in-Publication Data is available upon request.
Cover illustration: David Newton

ISBN 978-1-912453-45-0 (hardback)
ISBN 978-1-912453-00-9 (paperback)
ISBN 978-1-912453-15-3 (e-book)

Notice
The information in this book is designed to orientate readers of the work under analysis,
to elucidate and contextualise its key ideas and themes, and to aid in the development
of critical thinking skills. It is not meant to be used, nor should it be used, as a
substitute for original thinking or in place of original writing or research. References and
notes are provided for informational purposes and their presence does not constitute
endorsement of the information or opinions therein. This book is presented solely for
educational purposes. It is sold on the understanding that the publisher is not engaged
to provide any scholarly advice. The publisher has made every effort to ensure that
this book is accurate and up-to-date, but makes no warranties or representations with
regard to the completeness or reliability of the information it contains. The information
and the opinions provided herein are not guaranteed or warranted to produce particular
results and may not be suitable for students of every ability. The publisher shall not be
liable for any loss, damage or disruption arising from any errors or omissions, or from
the use of this book, including, but not limited to, special, incidental, consequential or
other damages caused, or alleged to have been caused, directly or indirectly, by the
information contained within.

CONTENTS

THE MACAT LIBRARY

The Macat Library is a series of unique academic explorations of seminal works in the humanities and social sciences – books and papers that have had a significant and widely recognised impact on their disciplines. It has been created to serve as much more than just a summary of what lies between the covers of a great book. It illuminates and explores the influences on, ideas of, and impact of that book. Our goal is to offer a learning resource that encourages critical thinking and fosters a better, deeper understanding of important ideas.

Each publication is divided into three Sections: Influences, Ideas, and Impact. Each Section has four Modules. These explore every important facet of the work, and the responses to it.

This Section-Module structure makes a Macat Library book easy to use, but it has another important feature. Because each Macat book is written to the same format, it is possible (and encouraged!) to cross-reference multiple Macat books along the same lines of inquiry or research. This allows the reader to open up interesting interdisciplinary pathways.

To further aid your reading, lists of glossary terms and people mentioned are included at the end of this book (these are indicated by an asterisk [*] throughout) – as well as a list of works cited.

Macat has worked with the University of Cambridge to identify the elements of critical thinking and understand the ways in which six different skills combine to enable effective thinking.
Three allow us to fully understand a problem; three more give us the tools to solve it. Together, these six skills make up the **PACIER** model of critical thinking. They are:

ANALYSIS – understanding how an argument is built
EVALUATION – exploring the strengths and weaknesses of an argument
INTERPRETATION – understanding issues of meaning

CREATIVE THINKING – coming up with new ideas and fresh connections
PROBLEM-SOLVING – producing strong solutions
REASONING – creating strong arguments

To find out more, visit **WWW.MACAT.COM.**

CRITICAL THINKING AND "DISTANCE STILL MATTERS"

Primary critical thinking skill: EVALUATION
Secondary critical thinking skill: PROBLEM SOLVING

A core objective of Pankaj Ghemawat's work is to present a critical approach to the accepted view of globalization. The prevailing opinion in the business world at the time of publication was that globalization was a positive force, bringing new opportunities to companies expanding globally. Evaluating this worldview against real cases of failed expansion attempts, Ghemawat points out that the dominant view of globalization does not allow us to understand the reason for these failures. He argues that an overlooked factor, distance between countries, creates additional risks and costs for companies when they enter a foreign market. Ghemawat cautions against over-optimism, and calls for a more holistic picture of globalization.

Ghemawat builds this argument by outlining an important practical problem: he points out that the existing analytical tools that managers use do not allow them to see the potential problems that their international expansion may face. He cites a case of how using a popular analysis tool, Country Portfolio Analysis, focuses managers' attention only on potential profits, overlooking costs. After highlighting this problem, he proposes a solution: the CAGE Distance Framework, an analytical tool that takes distance between countries into account, providing managers with the opportunity to see the potential pitfalls of their expansion, and uncover new opportunities where the balance between benefits and risks is better. This approach to identifying problems and providing solutions not only makes the article very vivid, but also demonstrates that using the critical thinking skill of problem solving may lead to novel solutions that improve existing business practices.

ABOUT THE AUTHOR OF THE ORIGINAL WORK

Pankaj Ghemawat is a renowned scholar of globalization who, at 23, became the youngest person ever to be appointed a full professor at Harvard Business School. Currently, he holds professorial positions at Stern School of Business at New York University and IESE Business School in Spain.

Ghemawat's work has inspired an array of recent research. Recognizing his contribution, *The Economist* included Ghemawat in its 2008 guide to the greatest management thinkers of all time.

ABOUT THE AUTHORS OF THE ANALYSIS

Alessandro Giudici is Lecturer in Strategy at Cass Business School, City, University of London. His research focuses on how organizations can support innovation dispersed across international contexts. His work has been published in outlets such as the *Academy of Management Journal, Strategic Organization, Long Range Planning*, and *Business History*.

Marianna Rolbina is a PhD candidate at Cass Business School, City, University of London. Her research is in management and strategy, with a particular focus on cultural industries.

ABOUT MACAT

GREAT WORKS FOR CRITICAL THINKING

Macat is focused on making the ideas of the world's great thinkers accessible and comprehensible to everybody, everywhere, in ways that promote the development of enhanced critical thinking skills.

It works with leading academics from the world's top universities to produce new analyses that focus on the ideas and the impact of the most influential works ever written across a wide variety of academic disciplines. Each of the works that sit at the heart of its growing library is an enduring example of great thinking. But by setting them in context – and looking at the influences that shaped their authors, as well as the responses they provoked – Macat encourages readers to look at these classics and game-changers with fresh eyes. Readers learn to think, engage and challenge their ideas, rather than simply accepting them.

'Macat offers an amazing first-of-its-kind tool for interdisciplinary learning and research. Its focus on works that transformed their disciplines and its rigorous approach, drawing on the world's leading experts and educational institutions, opens up a world-class education to anyone.'

Andreas Schleicher
Director for Education and Skills, Organisation for Economic
Co-operation and Development

'Macat is taking on some of the major challenges in university education ... They have drawn together a strong team of active academics who are producing teaching materials that are novel in the breadth of their approach.'

Prof Lord Broers,
former Vice-Chancellor of the University of Cambridge

'The Macat vision is exceptionally exciting. It focuses upon new modes of learning which analyse and explain seminal texts which have profoundly influenced world thinking and so social and economic development. It promotes the kind of critical thinking which is essential for any society and economy. This is the learning of the future.'

Rt Hon Charles Clarke, former UK Secretary of State for Education

'The Macat analyses provide immediate access to the critical conversation surrounding the books that have shaped their respective discipline, which will make them an invaluable resource to all of those, students and teachers, working in the field.'

Professor William Tronzo, University of California at San Diego

WAYS IN TO THE TEXT

KEY POINTS

- Pankaj Ghemawat is an Indian-American management thinker who has made major contributions to the research of globalization.*

- "Distance Still Matters" makes the argument that firms must look beyond countries' sales potential, at the impact that physical distance can have.

- "Distance Still Matters" provides a novel and useful analytical framework to assess the risks of doing business internationally.

Who Is Pankaj Ghemawat?

Pankaj Ghemawat is an influential scholar of globalization. His interest in the topic is fueled by his international background. Born in India in 1959, he went to the United States to study at Harvard University at the age of 16. After graduation, he worked in the United Kingdom for the renowned consulting firm McKinsey & Company. Continuing on this international path, Ghemawat now holds professorial positions at both New York University's Stern School of Business and IESE Business School in Spain.

Ghemawat's work focuses on the problems businesses experience when expanding globally. He challenges the widely held view that globalization is a universal, positive force, pointing out the multifaceted nature of this phenomenon. The increase in foreign direct investment* at the end of the 20th century led both practitioners and academics to look at the prospects of globalization over-optimistically. Ghemawat argues against such simplification, pointing out risks and costs associated with international expansion. Apart from his scholarly work, Ghemawat also collaborates with DHL* on its annual Global Connectedness Index.* He himself developed the index to inform management practitioners of international trends, beginning in 2011.

*Harvard Business Review's Thinkers50** ranked Ghemawat among the top twenty most influential management thinkers worldwide, for his contribution to the theory of multinational enterprise, as well as his impact on practitioners and policy makers. *The Economist* included him in its 2008 guide to the greatest management thinkers, the youngest "guru" to be included in this prestigious ranking.

What Does "Distance Still Matters" Say?

"Distance Still Matters," published in 2001, was a milestone in Ghemawat's academic career, and is one of the most important articles ever to be published in the field of international management. It uncovers a key reason why companies expanding internationally may fail, even when they choose to enter the markets that seem most profitable. The most significant reason, Ghemawat argues, is the fact that traditional tools, such as Country Portfolio Analysis,* focus only on the potential benefits of expansion, and disregard possible hindrances firms may face when entering foreign markets. In the author's view, traditional analysis methods lead managers to overlook the impact of international distance. Ghemawat sees this notion as more than simply a physical distance between two countries and presents distance as a multifaceted concept incorporating differences between countries in cultural, administrative, geographic, and economic spheres.

The main focus and key contribution of "Distance Still Matters" is a new tool—the CAGE Distance Framework—that allows managers to account for risks associated with cultural, administrative, geographic, and economic distance between countries when considering international expansion. The framework includes the attributes that constitute each dimension of distance, as well as a list of industries that are affected by distance when expanding internationally.

In "Distance Still Matters," Ghemawat systematically explains his novel understanding of distance. He provides examples of each dimension of this notion and explains how they impact different industries, highlighting which industries are more or less sensitive to each type of distance. For example, cultural dimension of distance includes norms, language and traditions, and strongly affects exports of cultural products such as television, as well as food exports. Administrative differences such as political hostility and different monetary systems affect firms exploiting natural resources. Geographic distance that incorporates the differences in countries' size and location creates difficulties for companies dealing with financial and other services where connectivity is important. Finally, economic distance that refers to differences in income and available resources, may impact firms demand for whose products varies with income level, such as the automotive industry. He also evaluates two compelling cases, which demonstrate that disregarding the challenges posed by international distance may lead to a failed expansion, while accounting for them may highlight opportunities that were previously overlooked.

The CAGE Distance Framework retains its relevance today, since international distance is an ever more important part of business, and companies must consider it when expanding internationally. The usefulness of the framework has been confirmed by its practical application, for example in adjusting companies' risk assessments and Net Present Value* calculations.[1] Furthermore, "Distance Still

11

Matters" has gained wide acceptance in academic circles, with over 500 citations on Thomson Reuters ISI Web of Science[2] and 1800 Google Scholar citations to date.[3] Furthermore, in the years since the article's publication, many scholars, such as Oscar Martín Martín* and Rian Drogendijk,* have expanded on the concept of distance by developing scales to measure its dimensions.

Why Does "Distance Still Matters" Matter?

The theory of multinational enterprise is a vast academic field that started with Peter Buckley* and Mark Casson's* seminal work *The Future of the Multinational Enterprise*, and has continued developing since. "Distance Still Matters" was a major contribution to this debate. It is written in a vivid style characteristic of *Harvard Business Review* publications, which makes it easily understandable to non-experts. It uses a variety of real life cases and lay language to transmit its key points. Thus, the article is a good entry point for students of other disciplines into scholarly writing on international business and the theory of multinational enterprise. The article, while short, gives a comprehensive account of related issues that are still very relevant for practitioners and policy makers and constitutes a research agenda for international business scholars.

For a modern reader used to instant communication and easy transportation, "Distance Still Matters" serves as a useful reminder that the world is not fully globalized, and understanding the differences between countries is crucial when companies consider global expansion. These differences play a significant role in determining companies' success or failure in entering foreign markets. Furthermore, they can help us understand why certain groups of countries trade with each other more or less intensively—the phenomenon known as regionalization dynamics*—as the DHL Global Connectedness Index shows.

The relevance of the ideas expressed in "Distance Still Matters" has increased in recent years, with major sociopolitical and economic events such as the Global Financial Crisis* and Brexit* raising concerns over the future of globalization. The previous, over-optimistic stance has given way to cautions that the world is becoming ever more fragmented, with some practitioners,[4] as well as scholars such as Alan Rugman,* even fearing the end of globalization.[5] However, as Ghemawat himself remarked in later works, both stances are exaggerated. "Distance Still Matters" provides a balanced view of global expansion, not denying the benefits a company may gain from becoming multinational, but at the same time calling for a careful analysis and consideration of all factors, both positive and negative, that may affect business. Adopting this point of view may help readers to think critically about globalization dynamics and consider how the distance between countries impacts international business.

NOTES

1   Robert M. Salomon, *Global Vision: How Companies Can Overcome the Pitfalls of Globalization* (New York: Palgrave Macmillan, 2016).

2   Search term "Distance Still Matters," *Web of Science*, accessed October 20, 2017.
    https://apps.webofknowledge.com/full_record.do?product=WOS&search_mode=GeneralSearch&qid=3&SID=C6yvoy6nVHcouLE5d7K&page=1&doc=1&cacheurlFromRightClick=no.

3   Search term "Distance Still Matters." *Google Scholar*, accessed October 20, 2017. https://scholar.google.com/scholar?hl=ru&as_sdt=0,5&q=distance+still+matters.

4   Ceri Parker, "The end of globalization? Davos disagrees," *World Economic Forum,* January 20, 2017, accessed November 20, 2017. https://www.weforum.org/agenda/2017/01/the-end-of-globalization-davos-disagrees/.

5   Alan Rugman, *The End of Globalization* (Random House Business Books, 2012), accessed November 25, 2017. https://www.penguin.co.uk/books/1046014/the-end-of-globalization/.

SECTION 1
INFLUENCES

MODULE 1
THE AUTHOR AND THE
HISTORICAL CONTEXT

KEY POINTS

- Ghemawat's work is part of a debate about the role and prospects of globalization sparked by the increase in direct foreign investment.
- "Distance Still Matters" challenges the traditional view by pointing out that globalization is hindered by the distance between countries.
- Ghemawat's life and work experiences in India, Europe, and America influenced his rejection of the idea of a "flat" globalized world.

Why Read This Text?

Pankaj Ghemawat's "Distance Still Matters" is a seminal work in the fields of international management and theory of multinational enterprise. Its key contribution is its discussion of cultural, administrative, geographic, and economic distance between countries as the main cause of additional costs, obstacles, and risks that companies face when expanding into new foreign markets.

In this work, the author calls into question simplicity and over-optimism regarding globalization. Ghemawat critiques traditional analytical tools, such as Country Portfolio Analysis, that focus solely on the potential benefits companies stand to gain from a particular foreign market. Instead, Ghemawat proposes a new tool—the CAGE Distance Framework—that incorporates the impact of distance and its potential negative effects on expanding firms.

> ❝ [Pankaj Ghemawat] is one of the younger representatives of the Indian gurus of management— men who straddle cultures, American, European and Asian, and throw new light on corporate behaviour, and particularly its global aspect. ❞
>
> *"Guru: Pankaj Ghemawat," The Economist*

"Distance Still Matters" was published in 2001, in the wake of a sharp rise in foreign direct investments across the world,[1] and the resulting enthusiasm about the prospects of globalization among business practitioners and media. The article aimed to provide a more balanced view of the phenomenon. Gemawhat's approach highlights the risks associated with global expansion as particularly relevant in the light of recent political, economic, and social events affecting globalization such as the Global Financial Crisis, or independence movements in Europe (for instance, in Scotland and Catalonia).

Author's Life

Pankaj Ghemawat was born in Jodhpur, India in 1959. From a young age, he experienced academic success. At fifteen, he graduated from secondary school and prepared for college. He first enrolled in an Indian university, but then transferred to Harvard University at the age of sixteen. At nineteen, he was accepted into Harvard's PhD program in Business Economics, which he finished three years later.

Upon completing his doctorate, Ghemawat spent one year in London. There, he worked for the consulting firm McKinsey & Company, before returning to Harvard to launch his academic career. Ghemawat joined the faculty at the Harvard Business School in 1983,[2] at the unusually young age of 23, and in 1991 he became the youngest person in the university's history to be appointed a full professor.[3] Since then, Ghemawat has written numerous journal articles, case studies and books on international business.

The emphasis on distance typical of Ghemawat's work is rooted in his wide international work experience in India, the US, and Europe. In 2008, he joined the prestigious IESE Business School in Spain. Currently, he holds professorial positions there and at NYU's Stern School of Business.

Ghemawat's affiliations with these two influential business schools have generated reciprocal benefits in terms of his reputation and the dissemination of his ideas. He has developed a confident stage persona by participating in many public and media talks around the world. Leveraging the two schools' publication resources, Ghemawat has released several books in recent years. These include *Strategy and the Business Landscape* in 2009; *World 3.0: Global Prosperity and How to Achieve It* in 2011; and his latest book, *The Laws of Globalization and Business Applications* in 2016.

Author's Background

With "Distance Still Matters," Ghemawat contributed to the debate on globalization which was prominent at the turn of the 21st century, thanks in particular to popular confidence in modern technological advancements. At the time, globalization was widely seen as a pervasive and unstoppable trend "by which the peoples of the world [would be] incorporated into a single world society,"[4] with technological advancement as its most powerful engine. A sharp decline in transport and communication costs and the growing adoption of the internet and e-commerce were pushing entrepreneurs and managers to internationalize.[5] The collective rhetoric shaped by media, consultants, and academics suggested that countries, markets, and cultures were becoming closer than ever before. Companies and consumers also shared the perception that markets were becoming more homogeneous and borders blurred.

Within this intellectual environment, Ghemawat argued that the seemingly never-ending opportunities created by globalization were being over-emphasized. He highlighted how prior analyses generally highlighted the positive aspects of international expansion but downplayed and substantially underestimated the real costs of doing business internationally. In his view, recognizing that countries and markets differ in terms of cultural, administrative, geographic, and economic attributes was still crucial in internationalizing business successfully.

In Ghemawat's view, "strategies that presume complete global integration tend to place far too much emphasis on international standardization and scalar expansion."[6] This stance stood in sharp contrast to mainstream voices of the time, such as that of Thomas Friedman,* who consistently supported a strictly positive characterization of globalization processes. Ghemawat argued, and indeed demonstrated, that in fact considerable cross-country barriers remained. Ghemawat's work is especially relevant today, due to an anti-globalization backlash that is making multinationals reconsider their business strategies and is raising concerns that "the biggest business idea of the past three decades is in deep trouble."[7]

NOTES

1   Angus Maddison, *Monitoring the World Economy: 1820–1992* (Paris: Development Centre of the Organization for Economic Cooperation and Development, 1995).

2   "Pankaj Ghemawat," *The Economist*, August 7, 2009, accessed November 13, 2017. http://www.economist.com/node/14201826.

3   "About Pankaj Ghemawat," *Ghemawat.com*, accessed November 13, 2017. https://www.ghemawat.com/about.

4   Martin Albrow, and Elizabeth King, eds, *Globalization, Knowledge and Society* (London: Sage, 1990), 8.

5   Thomas Friedman, *The World Is Flat: The Globalized World in the Twenty-First Century* (London: Penguin, 2007).

6   Martha Lagace, "Businesses Beware: The World Is Not Flat," *Working Knowledge*, October 15, 2007, accessed November 13, 2017, http://hbswk.hbs.edu/item/5719.html.

7   "The retreat of the global company," *The Economist, January 28, 2017,* accessed November 13, 2017, https://www.economist.com/news/briefing/21715653-biggest-business-idea-past-three-decades-deep-trouble-retreat-global.

MODULE 2
ACADEMIC CONTEXT

KEY POINTS

- "Distance Still Matters" builds on the "theory of the multinational enterprise," exploring the existence and nature of multinational enterprises.

- Ghemawat draws heavily on evidence within that literature to discuss the different dimensions of distance.

- By elaborating on the concept of distance, Ghemawat expanded on the work of Sumantra Ghoshal* on cross-border management.*

The Work In Its Context

In his PhD dissertation, Ghemawat argued against Thomas Friedman's thesis of a "flat," homogenous world. Ghemawat called this view "globaloney"* and suggested that companies should pay careful attention to regional differences when devising their global strategies. Most of Ghemawat's later work investigates the challenges of designing successful regional strategies.

Ghemawat's thinking in "Distance Still Matters" built on Peter Buckley and Mark Casson's "theory of the multinational enterprise." This body of work explored why multinational enterprises exist as organizational forms. The theory suggests that firms expand abroad in an attempt to make use of the arbitrage* opportunities presented by imperfect markets, for instance when having own operations* in a foreign country decreases the costs of international transactions. If markets are perfect, meaning there is no opportunity for firms to influence the price of their products abroad, there are no incentives to

> ❝ Essentially, international management is management
> of distance. ❞
>
> Srilata Zaheer* et al., *Distance without Direction*

expand internationally, and firms will remain within national boundaries.

Drawing on his international work experience, Ghemawat scrutinized the dominant view at the end of the 20th century that globalization offered endless opportunities. Condensing years of academic research and presenting his thoughts in lay language, "Distance Still Matters" intervened in the debate to argue that this position overstated the size of opportunities and underestimated "the costs of doing business internationally."[1] Using a rich variety of examples and case-study evidence, Ghemawat demonstrated systematically that the cultural, administrative, geographic, and economic distance across countries and between markets could still be decisive for international business success.

Overview of the Field

One of the major building blocks for Ghemawat's work was the theory of multinational enterprise, a research stream initiated by Buckley and Casson's seminal book *The Future of the Multinational Enterprise.* This work tied together different aspects of multinational operations to explain the existence of multinational enterprises and the contingencies that govern their expansion. It considered different types of international transactions, such as knowledge transfer, research and development costs, or tax liabilities, to point out that a firm expands internationally only if the benefits outweigh the costs. The academic discussion on globalization that Buckley and Casson provoked reached its peak in the early 2000s, when dozens of books and papers on the subject were published annually.[2]

The prevailing view at the time took globalization largely for granted, seeing it as an unstoppable force that would eventually lead to a uniform world. Supporters of this viewpoint, such as Thomas Friedman or Jeffrey Frankel,* tended to overlook national borders as a factor that might affect firms' international expansion. Frankel asserted that removal of financial control leads to integration and leveling of financial markets and elimination of country premiums.*[3] Essentially, he suggested that without additional taxation and controls that discriminate firms by country of residence, the world would become a unified economy where expanding internationally would be no more risky than expanding within a home country.

However, some counter-evidence suggested that this view oversimplified the complex issue of globalization. Increasingly, research on knowledge transfer* pointed out that distance was a barrier to knowledge spillovers.*[4] This means that the further apart two entities are, the more difficult it is for innovations in one to lead to innovations in another, slowing down the overall growth in productivity due to new technologies.

Furthermore, evidence on global trade suggested that the world was much less homogenous than the dominant view supposed. John Helliwel* observed that provinces of the same state trade with each other more intensively than with neighboring countries, even when the physical distance is the same, suggesting that national borders are not obsolete and have a significant role in global trade.[5] Ghemawat drew heavily on this contrary evidence to formulate his idea of semiglobalization,* which holds that there is an imperfect alignment of national markets, and different dimensions of distance can inhibit firms' global expansion.

Academic Influences
In "Distance Still Matters," Ghemawat develops his ideas on globalization with a business audience in mind—in particular,

managers, directors, and consultants. His work lies at the intersection of research on economic and international strategy and focuses on potential problems businesses encounter when expanding internationally. Ghemawat points out that, although modern technologies have increased levels of global connectedness, cross-country "distances" are still relevant to international business, and their associated costs and challenges are often underestimated.

Ghemawat developed this perspective by building on the so-called "theory of the multinational enterprise." This theory, introduced by Peter Buckley and Mark Casson, explains that companies expand abroad in order to make use of opportunities created by market imperfections in cases when the benefits of expansion, such as reduced tax burdens, efficient knowledge transfer, or cheaper production, outweigh the costs.[6] Ghemawat also drew from Sumantra Ghoshal's work on how firms achieve various objectives in their global strategy despite international differences.[7] He was influenced by C.K. Prahalad* and Stuart Hart's* work on how businesses can deliver value to poorer customers,[8] as well as Jeffrey Frankel and Andrew Rose's* scholarship on how different attributes of distance impact international trade.[9]

Ghemawat showed how international differences, explored by Frankel, Rose, and Ghoshal, act as a hindrance to exploiting the benefits of international expansion that were postulated by Buckley and Casson, but also uncover new opportunities to create value, as suggested by Prahalad and Hart. Ghemawat suggested that existing frameworks were overly positive in judging international business opportunities, ignoring the costs associated with important aspects such as cultural, administrative, geographic, and economic differences across countries and between markets.

NOTES

1   Pankaj Ghemawat, "Distance Still Matters: The Hard Reality of Global Expansion," *Harvard Business Review,* September, 2001, 138.

2   Search term "Globalization," *Google NGram*, accessed October 20, 2017. https://books.google.com/ngrams/graph?content=globalization&year_ start=1800&year_end=2.000&corpus=15&smoothing=3&share=&direct_ url=t1%3B,globalization%3B,c0.

3   Jeffrey. A. Frankel, "Measuring international capital mobility: a review," *American Economic Review* 82 (1992): 197-202.

4   Wolfgang Keller, "Geographic Localization of International Technology Diffusion," Working Paper No. 750, *National Bureau of Economic Research*, 2000.

5   John F. Helliwell, *How Much Do National Borders Matter?* (Washington, DC: Brookings Institution Press, 1998).

6   Peter J. Buckley and Mark Casson, *The Future of the Multinational Enterprise* (London: Macmillan, 1976).

7   Sumantra Ghoshal, "Global strategy: An organizing framework," *Strategic management Journal* 8 (1987): 425-440.

8   Coimbatore K. Prahalad, and Stuart L. Hart, "The Fortune at the Bottom of the Pyramid," *strategy+business* 26 (2002), accessed October 20, 2017, https://www.strategy-business.com/article/11518?gko=9a4ba.

9   Jeffrey Frankel and Andrew Rose, "An Estimate of the Effects of Common Currencies on Trade and Income," *The Quarterly Journal of Economics* 117 (2002): 437-466, doi: 10.1162/003355302753650292. Ghemawat cites an earlier, unpublished version of this article.

MODULE 3
THE PROBLEM

KEY POINTS

- "Distance Still Matters" focuses on how global expansion is impacted by cultural, political, administrative, geographic, and economic distance.

- Adding to our understanding of international differences, Ghemawat introduced the concept of distance between countries as the key factor.

- Ghemawat contributed to the theory of the multinational enterprise by laying the foundations for research into the actual state of globalization.

Core Question

In "Distance Still Matters," Pankaj Ghemawat addresses the question of why many companies struggle when pursuing global expansion. He sought to explain why companies "become so dazzled by the sheer size of untapped markets that they lose sight of the vast difficulties of pioneering new, often very different territories."[1] His analysis revolves around the concept of "distance," which encompasses cultural, political, administrative, geographic, and economic differences between countries. The concept of distance is then used to develop a novel analytic framework—the CAGE Distance Framework—that can assist managers in assessing such differences and their effects.

The ideas that Ghemawat presents in the article are part of his broader research agenda on what he calls "semiglobalization"—a condition "in which the barriers to market integration at borders are high, but not high enough to insulate countries completely from each

> ❝ [Ghemawat] refutes the idea that there is a single global economy...Instead, he argues, on the basis of various economic measures and indicators, nations are much more disconnected than we imagine. Regional differences exist and matter. ❞
>
> *Harvard Business Review's Thinkers50*

other."[2] In "Distance Still Matters" he explains how certain types of distance contribute to creating barriers to market integration. He supports his argument with evidence from a study published by economists Jeffrey Frankel and Andrew Rose, who estimated the extent to which international trade was influenced by different types of distance.[3]

Ghemawat's main insight is that "strategies that presume complete global integration tend to place far too much emphasis on international standardization and scalar expansion."[4] This built on other articles in which he pointed out how, for decades, Coca-Cola pursued a strategy based on significant standardization with the tagline "think global, act global," yet it ran into serious trouble at the end of the 1990s, mostly due to the Asian currency crisis.*[5]

The Participants
At the time when "Distance Still Matters" was published, the dominant view in the field was that globalization was an unstoppable force that would eventually diminish the differences between countries and create a perfectly globalized world. In contrast to mainstream thinking, Ghemawat argued that location and cross-country distance were still extremely critical for success in doing business internationally. He observed that most firms dangerously underestimated the real costs involved.

Ghemawat systematized the concept of distance and pointed out its different dimensions, building on prior research about the notion of international differences. In a 1994 article, "The Effect of National Culture on the Choice Between Licensing and Direct Foreign Investment," Scott Shane* found that cultural differences in trust guide the choice of foreign investment modes. Companies from countries with high trust tend to prefer licensing, while low trust country firms favor direct investment.[6] Similarly, Bruce Kogut* and Harbir Singh* had pointed out that cultural differences drive the choice of international entry strategies* as early as 1988.[7]

Management gurus such as Geert Hofstede* and Michael Porter* also had observed that countries differ from each other culturally in terms of the values people hold,[8] and economically in terms of propensity to innovate and employee mobility.[9] Such differences need to be taken into account by companies when moving from one country to another in order to avoid conflicts with the local consumers and execute their strategies successfully. In their seminal work *Managing Across Borders*, published in 1989, Christopher A. Bartlett* and Sumantra Ghoshal had expanded on the idea of glocalization,* noting that companies can choose to adapt to local requirements to varying degrees to better leverage the head company's and foreign subsidiaries' competences.

The Contemporary Debate

Ghemawat's theoretical connections to the wider academic debate on globalization can be traced in a related article published in the *Journal of International Business Studies* in 2003, "Semiglobalization and International Business Strategy."[10] Here, Ghemawat frames his research as a way to advance one specific postulate of Buckley's and Casson's "theory of the multinational enterprise," that "firms [seek to] maximize profit in a world of imperfect markets."[11] More specifically, Ghemawat observes that work building on this early insight has focused mainly on the same sources of market imperfection, such as "business/usage-specificity of key activities, resources, competencies, capabilities, knowledge, and so on, or their firm-specificity in the sense of being collectively held by the firm's managerial hierarchy or employee pool and inalienable from it."[12]

Ghemawat's main point is that previous frameworks have overlooked the possibility that key activities—such as production processes or knowledge transfer procedures—and resources—such as human capital or physical resources—that allow companies to create value are location-specific and cannot be found or created elsewhere. This means that firms tend to overestimate the expected benefits of globalized markets and substantially underestimate the costs.

Taken together, Ghemawat's two articles have sparked over a decade of research to determine the real development of the globalization processes. Dovev Lavie* and Stewart R. Miller* directly incorporated Ghemawat's notion of distance into an empirical study of alliance portfolio internationalization* in 2008, finding that as the distance between partners in an international alliance increases, firm performance decreases, then rises, and finally drops again.[13] More recently, Ilgaz Arikan* and Oded Shenkar* provided empirical support for Ghemawat's ideas: having analyzed data on international alliances, they showed that administrative distance in the form of animosity between countries is negatively associated with the number of alliances companies form between these countries.[14] In contrast, in a 2016 article, Alain Verbeke* and Christian Geisler Asmussen* employed the notion of distance to develop theory. They argued that region should be treated as a distinct unit of analysis, as the interconnectedness between different dimensions of distance leads to a sharp increase in the compound distance on regional borders, rather than a gradual increase from one country to another. [15]

NOTES

1 Pankaj Ghemawat, "Distance Still Matters: The Hard Reality of Global Expansion," *Harvard Business Review*, September, 2001, 138.

2 Pankaj Ghemawat, "Semiglobalization and International Business Strategy," *Journal of International Business Studies* 34 (2003), 139, doi: 10.1057/palgrave.jibs.8400013.

3 Jeffrey Frankel and Andrew Rose, "An Estimate of the Effects of Common Currencies on Trade and Income," *The Quarterly Journal of Economics* 117 (2002): 437-466, doi: 10.1162/003355302753650292. Ghemawat cites an earlier, unpublished version of this article.

4 Martha Lagace, "Businesses Beware: The World Is Not Flat," *Working Knowledge*, October 15, 2007, accessed November 13, 2017, http://hbswk.hbs.edu/item/5719.html.

5 Pankaj Ghemawat, "Globalization: The Strategy of Differences," *Working Knowledge*, October 15, 2007, accessed November 13, 2017, http://hbswk.hbs.edu/item/3773.html.

6 Scott Shane, "The Effect of National Culture on the Choice Between Licensing and Direct Foreign Investment," *Strategic Management Journal* 15 (1994): 627-642, doi: 10.1002/smj.4250150805.

7 Bruce Kogut and Harbir Singh, "The Effect of National Culture on the Choice of Entry Mode," *Journal of International Business Studies* 19 (1988): 411-432, doi: 10.1057/palgrave.jibs.8490394.

8 Geert Hofstede, *Culture's Consequences* (New York: Sage, 1980).

9 Michael E. Porter, "The Competitive Advantage of Nations," *Harvard Business Review,* March-April, 1990, 73-93.

10 Ghemawat, "Semiglobalization," 138-152.

11 Peter J. Buckley and Mark Casson, *The Future of the Multinational Enterprise* (London: Macmillian, 1976): 32.

12 Ghemawat, "Semiglobalization," 138.

13 Dovev Lavie and Stewart R. Miller, "Alliance Portfolio Internationalization and Firm Performance," *Organization Science* 19 (2008): 623-646, doi: 10.1287/orsc.1070.0341.

14 Ilgaz Arikan and Oded Shenkar, "National animosity and cross-border alliances," *Academy of Management Journal* 56 (2013): 1516-1544, doi: 10.5465/amj.2011.0210.

15 Alain Verbeke and Christian G. Asmussen, "Global, Local, or Regional? The Locus of MNE Strategies," *Journal of Management Studies* 53 (2016): 1051-1075, doi: 10.1111/joms.12190.

MODULE 4
THE AUTHOR'S CONTRIBUTION

KEY POINTS

- Pankaj Ghemawat advances the CAGE Distance Framework to assess the costs and obstacles in foreign market potential.
- Ghemawat suggests that conventional approaches such as those based on Country Portfolio Analysis provide an incomplete picture.
- With its unique focus on distance, Ghemawat's work represents a landmark contribution to the theory of multinational enterprise.

Author's Aims

In "Distance Still Matters," Pankaj Ghemawat's main aim is to provide an effective analytic tool to assist firms in their assessment of the potential risks and opportunities involved in expansion into new international markets. He first explains why country differences—specifically cultural, administrative, geographic, and economic factors—still represent a source of significant costs and difficulties. He then points out that many firms struggle when going international because they underestimate the costs of distance by using out-of-date analytic tools. Ghemawat criticizes one of these tools—Country Portfolio Analysis—in detail because of its excessive emphasis on potential sales and a general underestimation of the costs and risks of new markets.

Ghemawat dedicates most of the article to developing his novel framework—the CAGE Distance Framework—which, he argues, allows companies to conduct more thoughtful assessments of

> ❝ The idea is to help businesses cross borders profitably by seeing the world as it really is, rather than in idealized terms. ❞
>
> Pankaj Ghemawat, *Working Knowledge*.

internationalization costs. He details the framework's relevance systematically by using several short examples clustered around the framework's four country difference factors, mentioned above. He discusses cultural differences in terms of religious beliefs, race, social norms, and language; administrative differences such as political ties, protectionist measures, or legal systems; geographic differences in terms of the physical size of a target country, and its infrastructure and terrain; and economic differences related to wealth and consumer income. He argues that each represents a distinct form of distance between countries that needs to be adequately factored in by firms when assessing the potential of foreign markets.

Overall, Ghemawat's explanation is compelling, thanks to his engaging style aimed at practitioners rather than academics—an approach typical of the *Harvard Business Review,* where the article was published. In his writing, he is dedicated to warning business managers not to apply the frameworks he considers inadequate to the task of strategizing about international markets.

Approach

"Distance Still Matters" presents a novel analytic tool—the CAGE Distance Framework—designed to assist companies in assessing the attractiveness of foreign markets. Ghemawat builds this business rationale by recalling how much StarTV* struggled to enter the Asian market in the 1990s. He argues that its difficulties were caused by the inadequate analytic tools used by the company.

In typical *Harvard Business Review* style, "Distance Still Matters" presents a single key idea, composed of a challenge and a solution. The challenge is that, due to pro-globalization rhetoric and poor analytic tools, firms too often underestimate the real costs of doing business internationally. The solution proposed by Ghemawat, the CAGE Distance Framework, is an analytic tool that can support a more systematic assessment of how cross-country differences caused by cultural, administrative, geographic, and economic distance influence the chances of success in international markets. Ghemawat explains these different types of distance with useful real-life examples that make the framework easy to understand for business managers.

In Ghemawat's view, most of the tools available at the time underestimated the real costs of cross-border differences, wrongly assuming that a truly globalized world already existed. To demonstrate the usefulness of the CAGE Distance Framework, he shows how it could be applied to the case of Tricon Restaurants International,* a company that assessed the real potential of the Mexican market by including the effects of distance, as suggested by Ghemawat. To make this example more vivid, Ghemawat compares the use of the CAGE Distance Framework with the use of a conventional tool—Country Portfolio Analysis.

Contribution in Context

In the article, Ghemawat condenses in business-friendly terms the ideas on globalization that he develops more fully in another article, "Semiglobalization and International Business Strategy,"[1] published in the prestigious *Journal of International Business Studies* (*JIBS*). The latter piece is part of a broader research agenda on the concept of semiglobalization that he has developed at the crossroad of literature in economics and international business strategy. His main focus is on the so-called "theory of the multinational enterprise," developed by Buckley and Casson to explain how arbitrage opportunities drive the international expansion of firms, leading them to become multinational enterprises.[2]

In his *JIBS* article, Ghemawat is interested mainly in demonstrating that cross-border integration is incomplete, and outlines semiglobalization as a condition "in which the barriers to market integration at borders are high, but not high enough to insulate countries completely from each other."[3] Building on this contribution, "Distance Still Matters" details how different types of distance contribute to raising barriers to market integration. Ghemawat thus lays the foundations for a more advanced discussion on how such distances contribute to creating different arbitrage opportunities across international markets. He further develops this insight in another article in the *Harvard Business Review*, "The Forgotten Strategy."[4]

The unique focus on distance so acutely presented in "Distance Still Matters" is typical of Ghemawat's work and constitutes the cornerstone of his unique contribution since the late 1990s to the on-going debate about the pros and cons of globalization. Presented in a fresh and captivating writing style, the article is buttressed by plenty of interesting examples of each different type of distance. It also uses hard data based on the contribution of Jeffrey Frankel and Andrew Rose, who used econometrics* to explore how different attributes of distance impacted international trade.[5]

NOTES

1 Pankaj Ghemawat, "Semiglobalization and International Business Strategy," *Journal of International Business Studies* 34 (2003), 138-152, doi: 10.1057/palgrave.jibs.8400013.

2 Peter J. Buckley and Mark Casson, *The Future of the Multinational Enterprise* (London: Macmillan, 1976).

3 Ghemawat, "Semiglobalization," 139.

4   Pankaj Ghemawat, "The Forgotten Strategy," *Harvard Business Review,*
     November, 2003, 76-84.

5   Jeffrey Frankel and Andrew Rose, "An Estimate of the Effects of Common
     Currencies on Trade and Income," *The Quarterly Journal of Economics* 117
     (2002): 437-466, doi: 10.1162/003355302753650292. Ghemawat cites
     an earlier, unpublished version of this article.

SECTION 2
IDEAS

MODULE 5
MAIN IDEAS

KEY POINTS

- "Distance Still Matters" uncovers the impact of distance on firms' international expansion.

- Ghemawat advances the CAGE Distance Framework, demonstrating how it allows for considerations of distance in foreign market analysis.

- Written in a fresh and captivating style, the article illustrates different types of distance with a variety of interesting examples.

Key Themes

In "Distance Still Matters," Pankaj Ghemawat discusses why distances between markets are still significant for international business, despite the fact that modern technology has increased global connectedness. In Ghemawat's view, traditional approaches overstate the size of opportunities in foreign markets and "underestimate the costs of doing business internationally."[1] He argues that these costs relate to different types of distance and presents a comprehensive framework—the CAGE Distance Framework—to assess distance across four dimensions: cultural, administrative, geographic, and economic.

The article comprises three main sections. Ghemawat first builds the business rationale supporting his novel framework, recalling the challenges experienced by Star TV when entering the Asian market at the beginning of the '90s. He argues that, due to inadequate analytic tools such as Country Portfolio Analysis, Star TV become "so dazzled by the sheer size of untapped markets that they [lost] sight of the vast difficulties of pioneering new, often very different territories."[2] He

> ❝ Companies routinely exaggerate the attractiveness of foreign markets, and that can lead to expensive mistakes. ❞
>
> Pankaj Ghemawat, "Distance Still Matters"

supports his argument with empirical evidence from a recent study by economists Jeffrey Frankel and Andrew Rose, who estimate how different distance attributes impact international trade.[3]

In the second section, Ghemawat introduces the CAGE Distance Framework, discussing each basic dimension of distance—cultural, administrative, geographic, and economic—in detail. In the third section, the article concludes with a short case study of Tricon Restaurants International, showing how the company assessed the potential of the Mexican market—now one of its key trading arenas— by factoring in the effects of different types of distance. A traditional Country Portfolio Analysis, Ghemawat shows, would have led the company to abandon doing business in Mexico.

Exploring the Ideas

In "Distance Still Matters," Ghemawat suggests that too often firms focus on the positive aspects of international business opportunities and underestimate their real costs. Due to ineffective analytic tools, firms fail to appreciate the importance of cultural, administrative, geographic, and economic differences across countries and markets. With this insight, Ghemawat sought to challenge the contemporary mainstream view, put forth by scholars such as Frankel, Casson, and Buckley. They held that globalization was an overwhelmingly positive phenomenon "by which the peoples of the world [would be] incorporated into a single world society,"[4] providing internationalizing companies with plenty of risk-free opportunities. The main contribution of Ghemawat's article is a proposed comprehensive tool—the CAGE Distance Framework—to assess cultural, administrative, geographic, and economic distances across international markets.

In the first of the article's three sections, Ghemawat uses the challenges experienced by Star TV in its attempt to enter the Asian market in the early 1990s to substantiate the business rationale supporting his framework. Ghemawat argues that Star TV had assumed that consumer preferences in the new market were similar to their home American market, overlooking the cultural distance between the two regions.

In the second section, Ghemawat introduces his CAGE Distance Framework, explaining each dimension of distance in detail, with several real-life examples. He explains how cultural differences in religious beliefs, race, social norms, and language can be the source of substantial distance between two countries. He then argues that administrative distance can help or hinder international business, citing as examples political ties, such as those between Commonwealth* countries or among European Union* members, protectionist measures, and the quality of a country's institutional infrastructure, embodied, for instance, in its legal system. Next, he asserts that the geographic dimension is more than a matter of the physical distance between two countries, but involves other elements, such as the physical size of the target country, its access to waterways, and man-made attributes such as transportation quality and communications infrastructures.

To close the second section, Ghemawat shows that economic distance relates mostly to the relative wealth and income of consumers, because rich countries tend to attract more economic activity. He observes that companies pursuing economies of scale or experience may prefer to target countries with similar profiles because they can replicate their strategies more easily, whereas companies pursuing arbitrage opportunities may favor countries with less advanced profiles and likely lower labor costs.

In the article's third and final section, Ghemawat applies his framework to another case study—Tricon Restaurants International—demonstrating how this company evaluated the potential of the Mexican market by accurately including the costs of different types of distance. Traditional tools such as Country Portfolio Analysis would suggest that the best market to enter was China, because it has the most opportunities for profit. However, Tricon realized that the Chinese market would be too difficult to enter, due to the large distance between it and the US market. They therefore chose to enter the Mexican market instead. Although the projected profit was smaller, the entry costs and risks were also much lower, as the impact of distance was less.

Language and Expression

"Distance Still Matters" is written in *Harvard Business Review* style, with one main theoretical point—the proposed CAGE Distance Framework—supported by several examples to facilitate its dissemination among a practitioner audience, and an applied case to allow for replication in an academic setting.

Firstly, Ghemawat poses a problem, exemplified by the case of Star TV's attempted expansion into Asia: a firm's international expansion may fail, despite traditional analysis tools suggesting it will be profitable. He then suggests an explanation, namely failure to account for the costs and risks associated with differences between countries. Ghemawat makes his point vividly, explaining what different aspects of international distance entail and how they affect different industries in great detail. Finally, he proposes the CAGE Distance Framework as a solution to the problem he pointed out.

Presented in Ghemawat's fresh and captivating writing style, the article is supported by plenty of interesting examples of each different type of distance. The need for the CAGE Distance Framework is evidenced by the contrast between Star TV's struggle and Tricon

Restaurants' success. Ghemawat deploys these cases to illustrate both the dangers of not taking into account international distance in the analysis of new markets, and the opportunities that the CAGE Distance Frameworks helps to uncover.

NOTES

1 Pankaj Ghemawat, "Distance Still Matters: The Hard Reality of Global Expansion," *Harvard Business Review,* September, 2001, 138.

2 Ghemawat, "Distance Still Matters," 138.

3 Jeffrey Frankel and Andrew Rose, "An Estimate of the Effects of Common Currencies on Trade and Income," *The Quarterly Journal of Economics* 117 (2002): 437-466, doi: 10.1162/003355302753650292. Ghemawat cites an earlier, unpublished version of this article.

4 Albrow Martin and Elizabeth King, eds., *Globalization, Knowledge and Society* (London: Sage, 1990): 8.

MODULE 6
SECONDARY IDEAS

KEY POINTS

- In "Distance Still Matters," Ghemawat unpacks four types of distance that affect firms' international expansion.
- The article highlights that different industries show different degrees of sensitivity to the four types of distance.
- Ghemawat's ideas have been very influential and have been further developed by a number of subsequent scholars.

Other Ideas

The importance of the concept of distance presented in Pankaj Ghemawat's "Distance Still Matters" lies not in its novelty, but in its systematic understanding. Though the idea that countries differ from each other was not new, Ghemawat's article proposed a comprehensive, multidimensional way to assess distance across countries. The author did not simply list the various ways in which countries differ from each other, but systematized them in four dimensions that he described in detail. This systematic approach gave credit to the concept of distance, encompassing all the differences countries may exhibit without attempting to simply enumerate them. It also made theory-level abstractions and generalizations possible, while still acknowledging the individual differences between countries.

An important point Ghemawat makes in "Distance Still Matters" is that the four types of distances have differentiated effects. The second part of the article argues that industries are not uniformly affected by distance, but rather show varying degrees of sensitivity towards each of

> ❝ It does seem useful to ask ourselves, 'Just how global are we?' before we think about where we go from here. ❞
>
> Pankaj Ghemawat, *TEDGlobal*

the four dimensions. Ghemawat highlights that industries dealing with linguistic content and values such as television or foods are strongly affected by cultural distance. Administrative distance has the strongest impact on state-supported industries; geographic distance becomes a deciding factor for communications and products that are difficult to transport; and economic distance affects businesses that depend on standardization or agile supply networks, such as those dealing with appliances.

Exploring the Ideas

Ghemawat starts by discussing how cultural features—such as religious beliefs, race, social norms, and language—can be the source of substantial distance between two countries. His examples include issues related to different languages in products having high linguistic content (such as TV programs); different ethnicities' attitudes to foods and tastes; different preferences in terms of car size or electrical standards; and different social norms, such as those related to alcohol consumption.

Next, Ghemawat looks at administrative differences, arguing that political ties, protectionist measures, and countries' institutional infrastructures are often sources of important cross-country differences. For example, Britain's closeness to the Commonwealth countries or the strong relationship between European Union members influences how such countries do business with one another. Common protectionist measures include "tariffs, trade quotas, restrictions on foreign direct investment, and preferences for domestic competitors in the form of subsidies and favoritism in regulation and procurement."[1]

Finally, national legal systems can facilitate or hinder international business, for instance in terms of regulations relating to drug development, the use of natural resources, and infrastructure projects.

With respect to geographic differences, Ghemawat clarifies that they are not simply a matter of physical distance between two countries. In his view, geographic distance also involves the size of a specific target market, access to waterways and the ocean, topography, and the quality of a country's transportation and communication infrastructures. He offers various examples of industries in which physical remoteness plays an important role—for instance, the cement business, due to its product's low value-to-weight ratio— in which products are fragile or perishable—such as glass or fruit and vegetables—or where the infrastructure is crucial—such as financial services, where communication and connectivity are vital.

Finally, Ghemawat highlights how economic distances are very closely related to cross-country relative wealth and consumer income, and how these attributes are important determinants of a country's capacity to attract economic activities. Examples of industries affected by this type of distance include those in which the level of demand varies with income levels, like the automobile industry; those in which economies of scale are important, such as mobile phone sales; or those in which labor and other factor cost differences are salient, such as the garment industry.

Overall, the wealth of examples and the application of the CAGE Distance Framework to the case study of Tricon Restaurants in the final section make the article compelling for practitioners interested in international business, despite its foundation in economic and business theory.

Overlooked

One of the reasons why "Distance Still Matters" is widely considered a seminal contribution to international business research is that it is a very straightforward piece of work. Written in clear *Harvard Business Review* style, and enriched by several examples complemented by two short case studies, the article communicates important ideas in language suited to business practitioners, academics, and students alike. Arguably, there are no neglected areas or theoretical points that require significant attention. Challenging the established thinking that considered global markets closer than ever at the end of the 20th century, Ghemawat points out that the real costs of doing business internationally are too often misunderstood, and therefore underestimated. These costs, he argues, arise from cross-country cultural, administrative, geographic, and economic differences whose role in keeping markets distant from each other deserves more attention. To help firms intent on globalizing to address these challenges, Ghemawat outlines his novel CAGE Distance Framework, which provides a more comprehensive and multidimensional way to understand the importance of cross-country differences in international expansion.

Ghemawat further developed the ideas he presented in "Distance Still Matters" in two articles entitled "Semiglobalization and International Business Strategy"[2] and "The Forgotten Strategy,"[3] published in 2003 in the *Journal of International Business Studies* and in the *Harvard Business Review*. In the former, he provides a formal theoretical discussion, grounded in economic and international business theory, of why the degree of globalization was lower than many mainstream voices had confidently anticipated a decade earlier. More specifically, he demonstrated that cross-border integration was far from being complete, and that markets were therefore in a state of "semiglobalization," "in which the barriers to market integration at borders are high, but not high enough to insulate countries completely from each other."[4] In the latter article, he observed how different sources of cross-country distance could also generate unexplored opportunities for companies seeking to expand globally. Here, he extended the traditional economic concept of arbitrage to incorporate different types of distance as sources of price differentials between markets.

NOTES

1   Pankaj Ghemawat, "Distance Still Matters: The Hard Reality of Global Expansion," *Harvard Business Review,* September, 2001, 143.

2   Pankaj Ghemawat, "Semiglobalization and International Business Strategy," *Journal of International Business Studies* 34 (2003), 138-152, doi: 10.1057/palgrave.jibs.8400013.

3   Pankaj Ghemawat, "The Forgotten Strategy," *Harvard Business Review,* November, 2003, 76-84.

4   Ghemawat, "Semiglobalization," 139.

MODULE 7
ACHIEVEMENT

KEY POINTS

- Following publication, most opinion leaders agreed with Ghemawat's argument about the dangers of over-optimism regarding globalization.

- The examples Ghemawat provided of well-known companies and their struggles in international expansion were perceived as persuasive.

- While "Distance Still Matters" drew on relevant examples at the time of publication, its framework and concepts are still applicable today.

Assessing the Argument

Pankaj Ghemawat's insights into the importance of understanding the different dimensions of cross-country distance to the success of international business expansion have enjoyed widespread and long-lasting diffusion since the publication of "Distance Still Matters" in 2001. Ghemawat has further developed his insights in best-selling books for practitioner audiences, including *Creating Value Through International Strategy* in 2005; *Redefining Global Strategy* and *Crossing Borders in a World Where Differences Still Matter* in 2007; and *Strategy and the Business Landscape* in 2009. In his book *World 3.0: Global Prosperity and How to Achieve It,* published in 2011, he called for regulatory changes in support of a more sustainable globalization.

Nowadays, most opinion-leaders, academics, and journalists tend to agree that the confidence in the benefits of globalization commonly expressed at the end of the 20th century was at best overemphasized, because most analytic tools tended to underestimate

> **❝** In the last few years, Pankaj Ghemawat has embarked on a much needed crusade to document the actual depth and breadth of [the] globalization process. The picture that emerges from this academic endeavor is much more nuanced that the one often portrayed in the literature. **❞**
>
> Pol Antràs,* *Review of The Laws of Globalization and Business Application*

its costs. The relevance of Ghemawat's ideas has also increased over time due to the new challenges created by the Global Financial Crisis and the widespread social unrest of the last decade. As Ghemawat empirically demonstrated in 2016, the world is in fact now less globally connected than it was in 2007, capital markets are fragmenting and service trade is stagnant.[1] This evidence, collected in collaboration with DHL with the aim of providing longitudinal data on the evolution of globalization, is part of the annual DHL Global Connectedness Index[2] and indicates how Ghemawat's seminal ideas in "Distance Still Matters" still show substantial relevance for the business world. Art Kleiner,* Editor-in-Chief of the magazine *strategy+business*, has said that "[this index] lays out a distinct path for every country, and more importantly, a rationale for why that plan makes sense, backed up by Pankaj Ghemawat's prescient theory of global economic health."[3]

Achievement in Context

In "Distance Still Matters," Ghemawat argues that cross-country distance is still very important to international business, despite the fact that transport and communication costs have substantially decreased thanks to technological advancements. He observes that many companies underestimate just how much cultural, administrative, geographic, and economic differences may impact the bottom line in their international exchanges. Ghemawat advances the CAGE Distance Framework to incorporate these cost variables systematically in the assessment of international opportunities.

The article is enriched by several real-life examples that allow Ghemawat to communicate his ideas easily to a target practitioner audience. Some of these examples refer to companies or situations that were very well-known at the time of the article: for example, Ghemawat starts the article with the case of Star TV's entry to the Asian market in the early '90s. This was a strong counter-point to Thomas Friedman's book *The World is Flat*, which built on companies' real experiences to make an argument in favor of globalization. By citing examples that contradicted the dominating narrative of a positive and unstoppable globalization, Ghemawat highlighted the multi-faceted nature of this phenomenon.

From a historical perspective, "Distance Still Matters" was a timely contribution to the discussion of globalization. Published in 2001, it coincided with the burst of the dot-com bubble,* which arose due to over-optimism regarding the Internet's ability to overcome the impact of distance. Another crisis that prompted the media and the general public to reconsider the positive view of globalization were the 9/11 terrorist attacks.* Previously, globalization was seen as a uniquely positive force that was erasing differences in the world, but these crises demonstrated that it is a much more complex phenomenon that poses risks as well as providing benefits.

Limitations

Ghemawat contributed to a discussion that started in the 1970s. Since then, the number of books and articles on the topic of globalization published annually has gone up,[4] suggesting that the discussion is still ongoing. Even today, there are many questions left to answer: some scholars research the social consequences of globalization, analyzing in which circumstances it counts as a positive phenomenon,[5] whereas others question the depth and breadth of globalization.[6] "Distance Still Matters" proposes a holistic view of globalization, as a phenomenon that poses risks as well as opportunities for companies. The article contributed to bringing some consensus to the field, putting forward a view that became widespread among both academics and practitioners. The article's main ideas are still relevant. As Ghemawat himself wrote in his book, *The Laws of Globalization and Business Applications*, "the law of distance is both persistent over time and applies broadly across different types of interactions."[7]

The audience to which "Distance Still Matters" was addressed was primarily composed of practitioners, so the article has generally been cited in support of broader considerations on how companies internationalize without making any direct adaptation. Most applications have been fairly consistent with Ghemawat's seminal ideas and, with the exception of a few recent studies, have incorporated his framework directly as part of hypothesis development,[8] offering very little extension of his theories.

NOTES

1 Pankaj Ghemawat and Steven A. Altman. "DHL Global Connectedness Index 2016," *DHL*, accessed November 13, 2017. http://www.dhl.com/en/about_us/logistics_insights/studies_research/global_connectedness_index/global_connectedness_index.html#.VFff5MkpXuM.

2 Pankaj Ghemawat and Steven A. Altman. "DHL Global Connectedness Index 2012," *DHL*, accessed November 13, 2017. http://www.dhl.com/content/dam/flash/g0/gci_2012/download/dhl_gci_2012_complete_study.pdf.

3 Ghemawat and Altman, "DHL Global Connectedness Index 2012," 269.

4 Search term "Globalization," *Google NGram*, accessed October 20, 2017. https://books.google.com/ngrams/graph?content=globalization&year_start=1800&year_end=2.000&corpus=15&smoothing=3&share=&direct_url=t1%3B,globalization%3B,c0.

5 Joanna Tochman Campbell et al., "Multinationals and corporate social responsibility in host countries: Does distance matter?" *Journal of International Business Studies* 43 (2012): 84-106, doi: 10.1057/jibs.2011.45.

6 Alan Rugman, *The End of Globalization* (Random House Business Books, 2012), accessed November 25, 2017, https://www.penguin.co.uk/ books/1046014/the-end-of-globalization/

7 Pankaj Ghemawat, *The Laws of Globalization and Business Applications* (Cambridge: Cambridge University Press, 2016): 150.

8 E.g. Dovev Lavie and Stewart R. Miller, "Alliance Portfolio Internationalization and Firm Performance," *Organization Science* 19 (2008): 623-646; Eric W. L. Tsang and Paul S. L. Yip, "Economic Distance and the Survival of Foreign Direct Investments," *Academy of Management Journal* 50 (2007): 1156-1168.

MODULE 8
PLACE IN THE AUTHOR'S WORK

KEY POINTS

- Imperfect globalization and distance are two themes that are central to Pankaj Ghemawat's entire corpus.

- Throughout his corpus, Ghemawat describes globalization as complex phenomenon and encourages avoiding over-optimism.

- "Distance Still Matters" has been widely cited in international strategy, marketing, and geographic studies.

Positioning

The theme of globalization permeates Pankaj Ghemawat's work. In "Distance Still Matters" and related publications, he argues that the world is not as flat as Thomas Friedman suggested in his bestselling book *The World is Flat*. If the world were truly flat (in the figurative sense of being economically and culturally homogenous), Ghemawat points out, foreign direct investments would have accounted for a far greater percentage of global investments than the mere 10% they represented at the time.[1] Arguing against Friedman's thesis, Ghemawat calls his view "globaloney," and suggests that global companies should pay careful attention to regional differences and modify their strategy accordingly. Most of Ghemawat's writing has been devoted to investigating the challenges of designing successful regional strategies while working within existing, and often inflexibly centralized, organizational structures.

The concept of distance has become another long-running theme in Ghemawat's research. In the academic article following "Distance Still Matters," "Semiglobalization and International Business Strategy,"

> **❝** Ghemawat is a bit of a boundary crosser himself, combining academic formality, pragmatic business sense, and a habit of wide-eyed inquiry in the face of other people's assumptions. 'I imagine him, like Galileo Galilei before the inquisition,' wrote Nikos Mourkogiannis in the foreword to *Redefining Global Strategy*, 'unable to keep from saying, But it does move around the sun!' **❞**
>
> Art Kleiner, *strategy+business*

he further highlights that globalization is not a uniform process and is stronger within regions than between remote countries. Ghemawat further argues against the popular assumption of disappearing boundaries in a book published in 2011, *World 3.0: Global Prosperity and How to Achieve It*. In that work, he uses hard empirical data to demonstrate that the world is not as globalized as is commonly believed.

In his most recent book, *The Laws of Globalization and Business Applications*, Ghemawat brings together his two most significant concepts, the law of semiglobalization* and the law of distance.* There, he discusses their impact on the globalization process and firms' international expansion, offering insight to both managers and policy makers.

Integration

Throughout his body of work, Ghemawat strives to shed light on different aspects of globalization, describing it as a multifaceted phenomenon rather than a strictly positive force. In books and articles aimed at both academic and business audiences, he shows that even under the influence of new technologies in communication and transportation, the world has not become "flat" and uniform, and that differences between countries still exist and have a strong influence on how multinational businesses operate. In this complex world, cultural, administrative, geographic, and economic distances are the key factors creating additional costs and risks for firms expanding globally.

Understanding the real impact of different facets of international distance has been one of the key focuses in Ghemawat's work for over a decade, from its introduction in "Distance Still Matters" in 2001 to the summative discussion in *The Laws of Globalization and Business Applications* in 2016. In this latest book, Ghemawat retraces the development of globalization across history to point out its uneven and oscillating nature. Drawing on real-life data, he also further unpacks the notion of distance, highlighting how its dimensions affect different industries and how companies can manage these differences. The book represents a pinnacle of the research that started with "Distance Still Matters" and "Semiglobalization and International Business Strategy."

Ghemawat's research addresses contemporary changes in international business and their role in shaping globalization. By reading the entire corpus of his works, a reader can observe how technological and social changes accelerate and inhibit globalization, which the author shows as a complex phenomenon, far from the uniform or linear process it is often assumed to be.

Significance

"Distance Still Matters" has become highly influential in international business research, and has been widely cited. For example, the Thomson ISI Web of Science database reports over 500 citations to date.[2] By their nature, international business studies lie at the intersection between economics, strategy, and marketing research, so Ghemawat's work has contributed to these fields too. Overall, his ideas have both benefited from and extended research into notions of how global strategies are created and pursued, along with a number of smaller themes, such as location choices for foreign subsidiaries, international mergers and acquisitions,* and cross-country opportunity exploration.

With respect to areas of influence, around a third of the citations that the article has received are from outlets which focus on international strategy, such as *Journal of International Business Studies*, *Journal of International Management*, and *Strategic Management Journal*. A few others are in journals more focused on general management, like *Academy of Management Review*, *European Management Journal,* and *Journal of Management Studies*.

Other citations have been scattered across a large number of journals in many disciplines. The article's main influence outside international business and management studies has been in marketing and planning/geography studies. Even there, however, the main focus has been on themes very close to international business research, such as international marketing orientation, or how to choose locations for collaboration. Taken together, this body of work elaborates on Ghemawat's key insight that "strategies that presume complete global integration tend to place far too much emphasis on international standardization and scalar expansion."[3] As Ghemawat often notes, a clear example of a company experiencing the challenges of global integration is Coca-Cola,[4] which, at the end of the '90s, was forced to abandon its traditional strong focus on standardization and move to a clearer recognition of the importance of regional differences.

NOTES

1   Angus Maddison, *Monitoring the World Economy: 1820–1992* (Paris: Development Centre of the Organization for Economic Cooperation and Development, 1995), quoted in Pankaj Ghemawat, "Semiglobalization and International Business Strategy," *Journal of International Business Studies* 34 (2003), 140, doi: 10.1057/palgrave.jibs.8400013.

2   Search term "Distance Still Matters," *Web of Science*, accessed October 20, 2017, https://apps.webofknowledge.com/full_record.do?product =WOS&search_mode=GeneralSearch&qid=3&SID=C6yvoy6nVHcou LE5d7K&page= 1&doc=1&cacheurlFromRightClick=no.

3   Martha Lagace, "Businesses Beware: The World Is Not Flat," *Working Knowledge*, October 15, 2007, accessed November 13, 2017, http:// hbswk.hbs.edu/item/5719.html.

4   Pankaj Ghemawat, "Globalization: The Strategy of Differences," *Working Knowledge*, October 15, 2007, accessed November 13, 2017, http:// hbswk.hbs.edu/item/3773.html.

SECTION 3
IMPACT

MODULE 9
THE FIRST RESPONSES

KEY POINTS

- "Distance Still Matters" was favorably received by most practitioners and academics, although some have challenged its precision and usefulness.
- Other researchers have supported Ghemawat's core concept by testing it empirically.
- "Distance Still Matters" has been incorporated into reading lists for international business courses at many universities.

Criticism

With "Distance Still Matters," Pankaj Ghemawat made a seminal contribution to international business research. The article's ideas kick-started a flourishing research agenda on "semiglobalization," which Ghemawat defines more fully in an article published in 2003.[1]

"Distance Still Matters" was mostly favorably received, both in the press and in academic circles, provoking relatively little criticism. Many practitioners and academics previously unconvinced by positive views of globalization adopted Ghemawat's definition of distance and the CAGE framework.

Whilst most researchers accepted that differences between countries still existed, some questioned the utility of distance as a measure of them. Oded Shenkar suggested an alternative concept of "friction," attempting to refocus on how entities from different countries interact, rather than on what separates them.[2] Anne-Wil Harzing* upholds Shenkar's viewpoint, proposing to focus on specific differences between countries instead of distance, so that unique features are not overlooked

> ❝ This is not about a snapshot, a '10 percent presumption' of integration at a moment in time. This is about trend lines and a scale of change brought on by these new technologies. ❞
>
> Thomas Friedman, *Foreign Policy*

by applying a standardized measure.[3] Among supporters of the idea of distance, Srilata Zaheer, Margaret Spring Schomaker,* and Lilach Nachum* point out the lack of specificity and directionality in the concept, calling for a more robust definition.[4]

"Distance Still Matters" sparked an intellectual debate between Ghemawat and Thomas Friedman, whose book *The World Is Flat* took a firmly pro-globalization stance. This debate continued for several years, with both media and academics comparing each side's arguments. John Jullens,* supporting Ghemawat's non-flat global model, nonetheless remarked that the debate is slightly exaggerated, as Friedman originally stated that the world was becoming more globalized, without implying that it was already uniform.[5] Jullens insists that this trend finds a reflection even in Ghemawat's data, and should not be overlooked. In his comparison of *The World Is Flat* and Ghemawat's subsequent book *Redefining Global Strategy*, Beheruz Sethna* also referred to this debate as a "straw man," since both authors acknowledge that the world is not "flat" and differences still matter.[6]

Responses

Ghemawat responds to criticism in his latest book, *The Laws of Globalization and Business Applications*, published in 2016. There, he defends the concept of distance, analyzing it along with his opponents' alternative concepts and main arguments. He points out that alternative terms, such as friction, are not neutral in their implied consequences, and are not as widely used as distance. Moreover, he argues that the concept of distance allows for a focus on regularities, whereas studying individual differences has only limited use, due to a lack of generalizability.

Ghemawat accepts Srilata Zaheer's abovementioned critique. Addressing the need for a more robust definition, he devotes a section to delineating the distinction between distance, similar concepts, and specific characteristics of countries. He concludes that the concept itself does not have significant flaws that would offset the benefits of using it in analysis.

An important element in Ghemawat's effort to diffuse his work is his ongoing campaign to contest the pro-globalization ideas put forward by influential *New York Times* columnist Thomas Friedman in the 2007 bestseller *The World is Flat*.[7] Although the debate mostly developed without direct confrontation, Ghemawat has nevertheless persistently challenged Friedman's views in many ways. In particular, Ghemawat argues against Friedman's suggestion that the Internet has eliminated national boundaries, pointing out that data exchanges still happen largely within countries rather than between them.[8]

In his book *World 3.0: Global Prosperity and How to Achieve It,* published in 2011, Ghemawat once again dispels pro-globalization assumptions, calling for improvements in regulation which could foster sustainable globalization processes. This book was praised by *The Economist*, which observed that it "should be read by anyone who wants to understand the most important economic development of our time".[9]

Conflict and Consensus

Public and academic reactions to "Distance Still Matters" have been mostly positive: it is now on the reading lists of most international business modules, and has received hundreds of research citations. To an extent, these positive reactions were sustained by the fact that many practitioners and academics were unconvinced by the mainstream view of globalization as a process that was intrinsically beneficial for international exchanges.

Ghemawat has expanded on his ideas in several articles and best-selling books, such as *Creating Value Through International Strategy* in 2005, *Redefining Global Strategy* and *Crossing Borders in a World Where Differences Still Matter* in 2007, and *Strategy and the Business Landscape* in 2009. He has collaborated with DHL since 2011, developing the DHL Global Connectedness Index,[10] which aims to provide annual evidence on the state of globalization.

Ghemawat's ideas were not empirically tested by others until 2008, when Dovev Lavie and Stewart R. Miller used them for a research study into alliance portfolio internationalization.[11] More recently, Ilgaz Arikan and Oded Shenkar used Ghemawat's work to assess how cross-border alliances were influenced by national distance in 2013[12] and Oscar Martín Martín and Rian Drogendijk introduced a measurement scale for cross-country distance in 2014.[13]

These independent results, together with those from the DHL index, have so far confirmed and reinforced Ghemawat's stance that "strategies that presume complete global integration tend to place far too much emphasis on international standardization and scalar expansion."[14] A clear example of this view, as Ghemawat reports in a number of his publications, is the substantial change of strategy of Coca-Cola at the end of the '90s.[15] The US company was forced to abandon its strong focus on standardization and its tagline "think global, act global" in favor of more emphasis on regional differences.

NOTES

1 Pankaj Ghemawat, "Semiglobalization and International Business Strategy," *Journal of International Business Studies* 34 (2003), 139, doi: 10.1057/palgrave.jibs.8400013.

2 Oded Shenkar, "Cultural Distance Revisited: Towards a More Rigorous Conceptualization and Measurement of Cultural Differences," *Journal of International Business Studies* 32 (2001):519– 535, doi: 10.1057/palgrave.jibs.8490982.

3   Anne-Wil Harzing, "The Role of Culture in Entry-Mode Studies: From Neglect to Myopia?" in *Managing Multinationals in a Knowledge Economy: Economics, Culture, and Human Resources*, eds. Joseph L. C. Cheng and Michael A. Hitt (Bingley: Emerald Group Publishing Limited, 2003): 75-127.

4   Srilata Zaheer et al., "Distance without Direction: Restoring Credibility to a Much-Loved Construct," *Journal of International Business Studies* 43 (2012): 18-27, doi: 10.1057/jibs.2011.43.

5   John Jullens, "Friedman versus Ghemawat - How Flat is the World Really?," *John Jullens Global Perspectives* (January, 2013), accessed November 29, 2017, http://www.johnjullens.com/show.php?NewsId=67.

6   Beheruz N. Sethna, "Ghemawat v. Friedman: Is the World Flat?," *Decision Line* 39 (2008), 25-31.

7   Thomas Friedman, *The World Is Flat: The Globalized World in the Twenty-First Century* (London: Penguin, 2007).

8   Pankaj Ghemawat, "People Are Angry About Globalization. Here's What to Do About It," *Harvard Business Review Digital Articles,* (November 2016), accessed October 26, 2017, https://hbr.org/2016/11/people-are-angry-about-globalization-heres-what-to-do-about-it.

9   "The Case Against Globaloney," *The Economist,* April 20, 2011, accessed October 26, 2017, http://www.economist.com/node/18584204.

10   Pankaj Ghemawat and Steven A. Altman. "DHL Global Connectedness Index 2016," *DHL*, accessed November 13, 2017. http://www.dhl.com/en/about_us/logistics_insights/studies_research/global_connectedness_index/global_connectedness_index.html#.VFff5MkpXuM.

11   Dovev Lavie and Stewart R. Miller, "Alliance Portfolio Internationalization and Firm Performance," *Organization Science* 19 (2008): 623-646, doi: 10.1287/orsc.1070.0341.

12   Ilgaz Arikan and Oded Shenkar, "National animosity and cross-border alliances," *Academy of Management Journal* 56 (2013): 1516-1544, doi: 10.5465/amj.2011.0210.

13   Oscar Martín Martín and Rian Drogendijk, "Country Distance (COD): Development and Validation of a New Objective Measure," *Journal of Small Business Management* 52 (2014): 102-125, doi: 10.1111/jsbm.12035.

14   Martha Lagace, "Businesses Beware: The World Is Not Flat," *Working Knowledge*, October 15, 2007, accessed November 13, 2017, http://hbswk.hbs.edu/item/5719.html.

15   Pankaj Ghemawat, "Globalization: The Strategy of Differences," *Working Knowledge*, October 15, 2007, accessed November 13, 2017, http://hbswk.hbs.edu/item/3773.html.

MODULE 10
THE EVOLVING DEBATE

KEY POINTS

- Ghemawat's concept of distance and CAGE Distance Framework have been used to analyze a variety of economic and sociopolitical issues.

- Development of precise measures for types of distance has become the main direction of the research sparked by "Distance Still Matters."

- Ghemawat still promotes his ideas through his acclaimed books and articles, and through their use in the DHL Global Connectedness Index.

Uses and Problems

The first attempt to use the ideas presented in Pankaj Ghemawat's "Distance Still Matters" empirically was in a 2005 article on technology's impact on multinational companies' motivations for foreign investment by Lilach Nachum and Srilata Zaheer.[1] They called "for more research on the various dimensions of distance […] and its implications for international business strategy".[2] In 2007 Eric Tsang* and Paul Yip* investigated the economic dimension of Ghemawat's CAGE Distance Framework, finding it significantly influenced the hazard rates of foreign direct investments.[3] Dovev Lavie and Stewart R. Miller incorporated the framework in their 2008 study of alliance portfolio internationalization.[4] More recently leading researchers such as Robert Salomon,* Zheying Wu,* Joanna Tochman Campbell,* Lorraine Eden,* and Miller again have extended lines of inquiry based on Ghemawat's work.[5,6]

> ❝ It would be a mistake to talk about the end of globalization: The 'rewind' button on a tape recorder shouldn't be confused with the 'off' button. ❞
>
> Pankaj Ghemawat, *Globalization in the Age of Trump*

Since 2001, Ghemawat has reinforced his position in a series of influential articles and books, such as *Redefining Global Strategy* and *Crossing Borders in a World Where Differences Still Matter*. In the public arena, Ghemawat has also engaged in a sustained intellectual debate with Thomas Friedman, who outlined his pro-globalization ideas in a book published in 2007.[7] To challenge Friedman's perspective systematically, Ghemawat published *World 3.0: Global Prosperity and How to Achieve It* in 2011. In the book, he translates the ideas proposed in "Distance Still Matters" into a variety of economic measures and indicators, showing that globalization is neither complete nor unstoppable. He also applies his ideas of distance and semiglobalization to sociopolitical issues, such as Brexit and Donald Trump's* election.[8]

It may be too early to judge whether many other researchers will engage with Ghemawat's ideas, enhancing and extending them. Although it is clear that "Distance Still Matters" and the CAGE Distance Framework are widely cited and referenced in the business world, as with other influential concepts,[9] more time is needed to verify the true extent of their broader intellectual influence.

Schools of Thought

Ghemawat's work in "Distance Still Matters," and his CAGE Distance Framework, have had considerable influence in the business world, thanks to their widespread adoption in countless international business study modules. They have also been positively received in academia, and extensively cited in international business research.

However, academic studies only started to test the framework in 2008, when Lavie and Miller used it in a study on alliance portfolio internationalization.[10] Their paper answered Nachum and Zaheer's 2005 call for more research on Ghemawat's framework. Eric Tsang and Paul Yip also empirically confirmed Ghemawat's findings, proving that economic distance significantly influences the hazard rates of foreign direct investments.[11] Similar supporting results have also been found by Robert Salomon and Zheying Wu in relation to geographic and institutional distance.[12] In 2012, Joanna Tochman Campbell, Lorraine Eden, and Stewart R. Miller expanded on Lavie's and Miller's contribution by employing Ghemawat's CAGE Distance Framework to study the effects of distance on how multinational companies conduct corporate social responsibility activities in host countries.[13] Their findings confirmed the predictions of the CAGE framework, showing that foreign affiliates from more distant home countries are less likely to engage in social responsibility practices than affiliates from closer home countries.

It is too early to judge whether Ghemawat's ideas will form an academic school of thought, but his work has already led to a greater appreciation of the importance of distance in the international business debate. As with other influential concepts, the intellectual diffusion of the CAGE Distance Framework is likely to gain momentum until a critical mass of contributions is achieved. At that point, new perspectives will be advanced, either challenging or substantially extending his work. Ghemawat himself is also likely to enrich his view with further contributions, as he has done in several books and articles over the last two decades.

In Current Scholarship

Ghemawat's contribution in "Distance Still Matters" has had a profound influence on both academic research and the public debate on international business and globalization. Cited hundreds of times, and included on the reading lists of many international business courses, the article has helped to shift the overwhelmingly confident view of globalization, creating a more balanced conversation.

Ghemawat has further developed the important insights of "Distance Still Matters" in subsequent books, including *Creating Value Through International Strategy* in 2005; *Redefining Global Strategy* and *Crossing Borders in a World Where Differences Still Matter* in 2007; *Strategy and the Business Landscape* in 2009; *World 3.0: Global Prosperity and How to Achieve It* in 2011; and *The Laws of Globalization and Business Applications* in 2016. This body of research was the principal reason *The Economist* included him in its influential guide to the greatest management thinkers of all time in 2008.[14]

At least two other *Harvard Business Review* articles—"The Forgotten Strategy"[15] and "Managing Differences,"[16] appearing in 2003 and 2007 respectively—have been widely influential in extending Ghemawat's line of work. In the former, he explores how cross-country differences might also offer novel international opportunities, explaining that cultural, administrative, geographic, and economic differences might represent sources of unexpected price differentials between foreign markets. In "Managing Differences," he presents the AAA Triangle Framework, designed to help managers and executives identify the most effective basic strategies for doing business internationally. He argues that the choice between "adaptation," "aggregation," or "arbitrage" strategies has profound organizational implications.

Finally, in collaboration with DHL, Ghemawat compiles the DHL Global Connectedness Index,[17] which condenses longitudinal data to show that countries and markets are much less connected than previously thought.

NOTES

1 Lilach Nachum and Srilata Zaheer, "The Persistence of Distance? The Impact of Technology on MNE Motivations for Foreign Investment," *Strategic Management Journal* 26 (2005): 747-768, doi: 10.1002/smj.472.

2   Nachum and Zaheer, "*The Persistence of Distance?,*" 764.

3   Eric W. L. Tsang and Paul S. L. Yip, "Economic Distance and the Survival of Foreign Direct Investments," *Academy of Management Journal* 50 (2007): 1156-1168, doi: 10.2307/20159917.

4   Dovev Lavie and Stewart R. Miller, "Alliance Portfolio Internationalization and Firm Performance," *Organization Science* 19 (2008): 623-646, doi: 10.1287/orsc.1070.0341.

5   Robert Salomon and Zheying Wu, "Institutional distance and local isomorphism strategy," *Journal of International Business Studies* 43 (2012): 343-367, doi: 10.1057/jibs.2012.3.

6   Joanna Tochman Campbell et al., "Multinationals and corporate social responsibility in host countries: Does distance matter?" *Journal of International Business Studies* 43 (2012): 84-106, doi: 10.1057/jibs.2011.45.

7   Thomas Friedman, *The World Is Flat: The Globalized World in the Twenty-First Century* (London, UK: Penguin, 2007).

8   Pankaj Ghemawat, "Globalization in the Age of Trump," *Harvard Business Review,* July-August, 2017, 112-123.

9   Alessandro Giudici and Patrick Reinmoeller, "Dynamic capabilities in the dock: A case of reification?" *Strategic Organization* 10 (2012): 436-449, doi: 10.1177/1476127012457977.

10 Lavie and Miller, "Alliance Portfolio Internationalization and Firm Performance."

11 Tsang and Yip, "Economic Distance and the Survival of Foreign Direct Investments."

12 Salomon and Wu, "Institutional distance and local isomorphism strategy."

13 Campbell et al., "Multinationals and corporate social responsibility in host countries."

14 Tim Hindle, *The Economist's Guide to Management Gurus and Ideas* (London, UK: Economist Books, 2012).

15 Pankaj Ghemawat, "The Forgotten Strategy," *Harvard Business Review,* November, 2003, 76-84.

16 Pankaj Ghemawat, "Managing Differences: The Central Challenge of Global Strategy," *Harvard Business Review,* March, 2007, 58-68.

17 Pankaj Ghemawat and Steven A. Altman. "DHL Global Connectedness Index 2016," *DHL,* accessed November 13, 2017. http://www.dhl.com/en/about_us/logistics_insights/studies_research/global_connectedness_index/global_connectedness_index.html#.VFff5MkpXuM.

MODULE 11
IMPACT AND INFLUENCE TODAY

KEY POINTS

- The ideas postulated in "Distance Still Matters" have spread, with practitioners seeing value in the adoption of a more nuanced view of globalization.

- Due to Pankaj Ghemawat's work, only a few researchers now argue in favor of seeing globalization as an irreversible and unstoppable force.

- Ghemawat argues that recent geopolitical changes demonstrate the dangers of overestimating the extent of both globalization and protectionism.

Position

The ideas Pankaj Ghemawat first presented in "Distance Still Matters" have enjoyed sustained diffusion over the last decade. At the time of the article's original publication, mainstream thinking saw globalization as an intrinsically beneficial and unstoppable process. Nowadays this confidence has been tempered, with most voices agreeing that we live in a world which is far from being truly globalized. The consequences of the financial crisis and the last few years of widespread social unrest have had an impact on how people think about globalization.

The Global Connectedness Index, on which Ghemawat has collaborated with DHL since 2011, has been very influential in the business world, due to its important managerial implications. The former Director-General of the World Trade Organization, Pascal Lamy,* has stated that "in the current global economic climate where the threat of increased protectionism and isolationist tendencies is of genuine concern, [this index shows] why increased global and regional

> **"** Today's turmoil calls for a more subtle reworking of multinationals' strategies, organizational structures, and approaches to societal engagement. **"**
> Pankaj Ghemawat, *Globalization in the Age of Trump*

inter-connectedness and openness is the more prudent policy path on which to proceed."[1]

Although Ghemawat's insights on globalization are increasingly accepted, other influential voices—such as that of Thomas Friedman—continue to disagree, supporting a more pro-globalization perspective.[2] Ghemawat has engaged in an intense campaign to challenge Friedman's view on this issue. In his 2011 book *World 3.0: Global Prosperity and How to Achieve It,* he develops the ideas of "Distance Still Matters," using hard data—virtually absent from Friedman's work—demonstrating that the global recession has led many governments, economies, and societies to retrench and increase protectionist measures. The book suggests that such moves may prevent the realization of the true benefits of cross-border openness. Ghemawat calls for collaboration between businesses, policy makers, the media, and citizens to create regulated ways in which to maximize the open flow of ideas, people, and goods across borders.[3] *The Economist* praised Ghemawat's book, saying it "should be read by anyone who wants to understand the most important economic development of our time."[4]

Interaction

The current intellectual debate on globalization has been profoundly influenced by Ghemawat's ideas, and "Distance Still Matters" is his seminal contribution. Globally, a debate rages on how to constructively manage and drive globalization, particularly given the impact of the financial crisis and social unrest in many parts of the world. This debate goes beyond the boundaries of international business and is closely related to economics, as well as to political science, sociology, cultural studies, law, and other fields. It is clear that mainstream thinking is now more balanced: rather than seeing globalization as purely beneficial, or unstoppable, many voices agree that our world is far from fully globalized, and substantial cross-country barriers persist.

From the perspective of economic and international business research, Ghemawat is one of the most relevant participants in this debate. His concept of semiglobalization,[5]—the notion that globalization is very far from being complete or irreversible—is widely used in both academic and media conversations. Ghemawat has been influenced by other scholars' contributions, such as Buckley and Casson's "theory of the multinational enterprise,"[6] Sumantra Ghoshal's work on managing across borders, and C.K. Prahalad's investigations into how businesses can deliver value to poorer customers.[7]

Despite this shift in mainstream thinking, many proponents of the pro-globalization perspective remain, strongly articulating the view of globalization as a fundamentally positive, democratizing process. Ghemawat has actively challenged this stance, both as a writer and a speaker, communicating and refining his ideas in over 100 articles and books. Ghemawat presents compelling hard evidence to challenge Friedman's view that global differences are being eroded, with products and services looking increasingly similar across countries and competition becoming more and more global.[8] Ghemawat labels this view "globaloney," arguing that companies pursuing global reach should pay careful attention to regional differences, and the hidden costs generated by persistent differences of culture, geography, administrative frameworks and economic characteristics. This view has been positively received—*Strategy&* partner John Jullens concludes in *strategy+business* that "on balance, Ghemawat wins the argument hands down."[9]

The Continuing Debate

Ghemawat's insights into the importance of the different dimensions of cross-country distance to the success of international business have enjoyed widespread and long-lasting diffusion since the 2001 publication of "Distance Still Matters." The relevance of Ghemawat's ideas has increased over time due to the new challenges created by the global financial crisis and the widespread social unrest of the last decade. As Ghemawat empirically demonstrated in 2016, the world is in fact now less globally connected than it was in 2007, capital markets are fragmenting, and service trade is stagnant.[10] This evidence, collected in collaboration with DHL with the aim of providing longitudinal data on the evolution of globalization, is now part of the annual DHL Global Connectedness Index. It indicates that Ghemawat's seminal ideas still show substantial relevance for the business world.

The turbulent international situation gives further support to Ghemawat's idea of semiglobalization. In his latest *Harvard Business Review* article, "Globalization in the Age of Trump," published in 2017, Ghemawat draws readers' attention towards a UK and US shift to protectionism. Using the DHL Global Connectedness Index, as well as historical data, Ghemawat cautions against over-optimism about both globalization and protectionism, saying that the belief the world was becoming "flat," and the global economy would soon be dominated by multinational enterprise, has been proven wrong. "Today's cries for a massive pullback from globalization in the face of new protectionist pressures are also an overreaction, in the other direction." [11]

NOTES

1   Pankaj Ghemawat and Steven A. Altman. "DHL Global Connectedness Index 2012," *DHL*, 269. Accessed November 13, 2017, http://www.dhl.com/content/dam/flash/g0/gci_2012/download/dhl_gci_2012_complete_study.pdf

2   Thomas Friedman, *The World Is Flat: The Globalized World in the Twenty-First Century* (London: Penguin, 2007).

3   Pankaj Ghemawat, *World 3.0: Global Prosperity and How to Achieve It* (Boston, MA, US: Harvard Business School Press, 2011).

4   The Case Against Globaloney," *The Economist,* April 20, 2011, accessed 26 October 2017. http://www.economist.com/node/18584204.

5   Pankaj Ghemawat, "Semiglobalization and International Business Strategy," *Journal of International Business Studies* 34 (2003), 139, doi: 10.1057/palgrave.jibs.8400013.

6   Peter J. Buckley and Mark Casson, *The Future of the Multinational Enterprise (*London: Macmillan, 1976).

7   Coimbatore K. Prahalad and Stuart L. Hart, "The Fortune at the Bottom of the Pyramid", *strategy+business* 26 (2002), accessed October 20, 2017. https://www.strategy-business.com/article/11518?gko=9a4ba.

8   Thomas Friedman, *The World Is Flat: The Globalized World in the Twenty-First Century* (London: Penguin, 2007).

9   John Jullens, "The Flat World Debate Revisited," *strategy+business*, May 6, 2013, accessed 13 November, 2017. http://www.strategy-business.com/article/00190?gko=403fb.

10 Pankaj Ghemawat and Steven A. Altman. "DHL Global Connectedness Index 2016," *DHL*, accessed November 13, 2017, http://www.dhl.com/en/about_us/logistics_insights/studies_research/global_connectedness_index/global_connectedness_index.html#.VFff5MkpXuM.

11 Pankaj Ghemawat, "Globalization in the Age of Trump," Harvard Business Review, July-August, 2017, 112-123.

MODULE 12
WHERE NEXT?

KEY POINTS

- A number of scholars expanded on the CAGE Distance Framework, suggesting that the concept of distance has a development potential.

- According to Pankaj Ghemawat, future directions of distance-driven research should consider subjective understanding of distance.

- The diffusion of the ideas relayed in "Distance Still Matters" is due both to the topicality of the subject and Ghemawat's own active efforts.

Potential

The influence and relevance of Pankaj Ghemawat's "Distance Still Matters" and of the CAGE Distance Framework are likely to continue increasing in coming years. Research suggests that the diffusion of academic concepts usually takes at least a decade to gain momentum,[1] so the article's citation numbers will probably continue to grow. It is also reasonable to expect the pace of diffusion to increase once the number of studies that directly utilize the CAGE Distance Framework achieves a critical mass. The first to do so was a paper by Dovev Lavie and Stewart R. Miller in 2008, in which Ghemawat's framework was used to study alliance portfolio internationalization.[2] More recent examples include a paper by Ilgaz Arikan and Oded Shenkar on the role of distance in cross-border alliances (in 2013),[3] and another by Oscar Martín Martín and Rian Drogendijk, in which the authors introduce a measurement scale for cross-country distance (in 2014).[4] The concept of distance was also

> **❝** Clearly, there are many opportunities to further increase our understanding of distance and how it affects international business. **❞**
>
> Pankaj Ghemawat, *The Laws of Globalization and Business Applications*

employed in an article by Tatiana Kostova, Phillip C. Nell, and Anne K. Hoenen to theorize the different manifestations of a foreign subsidiary's agency (2016),[5] and by Alain Verbeke and Christian Geisler Asmussen to distinguish between the local, regional, and global reach of firm-specific advantages (in 2016).[6]

The diffusion of Ghemawat's ideas about the importance of cross-country distance has been sustained and reinforced by his own efforts. He has published many other articles since "Distance Still Matters," including the widely cited "The Forgotten Strategy" in 2003, and the more recent "The Cosmopolitan Corporation" in 2011, as well as books such as *Redefining Global Strategy* and *Crossing Borders in a World Where Differences Still Matter* in 2007, and the more recent work *The Laws of Globalization and Business Applications* in 2016.

Future Directions

Although the ideas proposed by Ghemawat in "Distance Still Matters" have grown considerably in influence in international business research, to date there has been very little debate about them. The first serious attempt to use Ghemawat's ideas empirically was an article on the impact of technology on multinational companies' motivations for foreign investment by Lilach Nachum and Srilata Zaheer published in 2005, which concluded with a call "for more research on the various dimensions of distance [...] and its implications for international business strategy."[7] Later Eric Tsang and Paul Yip established the effect of the economic distance dimension of Ghemawat's CAGE Distance Framework on the hazard rates of foreign direct investments.[8] More recently other leading researchers have further extended lines of inquiry based on Ghemawat's work.[9,10]

At the same time, Ghemawat has reinforced his position over the last few years in a series of other influential articles and in his best-selling books. In his latest book, *The Laws of Globalization and Business Applications,* Ghemawat points out six future directions for distance-driven research: unpacking the different dimensions of distance, mapping the distance landscape, elaborating on inter-industry variation, exploring the concept of distance within firms, considering the subjective aspect of distance, and gathering more empirical data to validate the measures of distance.[11]

Although it is clear that "Distance Still Matters" and the CAGE Distance Framework are widely cited and referenced in the business world, as with other influential concepts,[12] more time is needed to verify the true extent of their broader intellectual influence. It is very likely that the next few years will see a rise in the number of contributions testing and refining Ghemawat's framework until a critical mass is achieved, in concert with his own efforts to popularize and extend his work.

Summary

"Distance Still Matters" is a landmark in the last two decades of international business research. The article has been widely influential within the academic world, in public debate, and among practitioners. The core of Ghemawat's message is that firms too often pursue internationalization strategies in which the expected benefits of globalization—such as lower transport and communication costs, converging consumer preferences, and so on—are greatly emphasized, but where the costs are substantially underestimated. In Ghemawat's view, globalization is far from being either a fully complete or an unstoppable process, because substantial cross-country cultural, institutional, geographic, and economic differences still impact the cost of doing business internationally.

The successful diffusion and influence of "Distance Still Matters" has benefited from at least two factors. First, in an intellectual environment in which globalization was conventionally seen as an inherently positive and unstoppable process, Ghemawat was among the first credible voices to reach the wider business and academic audience that proposed an alternative, more cautious perspective. Not surprisingly, his emphasis on the weaknesses of standard analytic tools used to design internationalization strategies, and his proposal of a novel, more effective framework—the CAGE Distance Framework—resonated strongly with many firms that were struggling to successfully conduct business abroad. Second, Ghemawat has himself persistently pushed and further refined his ideas in several other articles and best-selling books over the last ten years, so reaching an even broader audience. In addition, he has also extensively engaged with its business audience using blogs, social media and TED talks. His views on globalization will no doubt continue to inform the changing economic landscape of our world.

NOTES

1   Alessandro Giudici and Patrick Reinmoeller, "Dynamic capabilities in the dock: A case of reification?" *Strategic Organization* 10 (2012): 436-449, doi: 10.1177/1476127012457977.

2   Dovev Lavie and Stewart R. Miller, "Alliance Portfolio Internationalization and Firm Performance," *Organization Science* 19 (2008): 623-646, doi: 10.1287/orsc.1070.0341.

3   Ilgaz Arikan and Oded Shenkar, "National animosity and cross-border alliances," *Academy of Management Journal* 56 (2013): 1516-1544, doi: 10.5465/amj.2011.0210.

4   Oscar Martín Martín and Rian Drogendijk, "Country Distance (COD): Development and Validation of a New Objective Measure," *Journal of Small Business Management* 52 (2014): 102-125, doi: 10.1111/jsbm.12035.

5   Tatiana Kostova et al., "Understanding Agency Problems in
    Headquarters-Subsidiary Relationships in Multinational Corporations:
    A Contextualized Model", *Journal of Management* 5 (2016): 1-27, doi:
    10.1177/0149206316648383.

6   Alain Verbeke and Christian G. Asmussen, "Global, Local, or Regional? The
    Locus of MNE Strategies," *Journal of Management Studies* 53 (2016):
    1051-1075, doi: 10.1111/joms.12190.

7   Lilach Nachum and Srilata Zaheer, "The Persistence of Distance? The
    Impact of Technology on MNE Motivations for Foreign Investment," *Strategic
    Management Journal* 26 (2005): 747-768, doi: 10.1002/smj.764.

8   Eric W. L. Tsang and Paul S. L. Yip, "Economic Distance and the Survival of
    Foreign Direct Investments," *Academy of Management Journal* 50 (2007):
    1156-1168, doi: 10.2307/20159917.

9   Robert Salomon and Zheying Wu, "Institutional distance and local
    isomorphism strategy," *Journal of International Business Studies* 43
    (2012): 343-367, doi: 10.1057/jibs.2012.3.

10 Joanna Tochman Campbell et al., "Multinationals and corporate social
    responsibility in host countries: Does distance matter?" Journal of
    International Business Studies 43 (2012): 84-106, doi: 10.1057/
    jibs.2011.45.

11 Pankaj Ghemawat, *The Laws of Globalization and Business Applications*
    (Cambridge: Cambridge University Press, 2016): *Chapter 7.*

12 Giudici and Reinmoeller, "Dynamic capabilities in the dock."

GLOSSARY

GLOSSARY OF TERMS

9/11: a series of four coordinated terrorist attacks by the Islamic terrorist group al-Qaeda on major United States cities that were carried out using hijacked planes on the 11th of September, 2001.

Alliance Portfolio Internationalization: an indicator that indicates how different from a firm its foreign partners are by measuring international differences between the firm's home country and its partners' countries.

Anti-globalization: a social movement that criticizes and opposes economic globalization. The movement argues that multinational enterprises abuse their economic power to gain political influence, disregard work safety regulations and environmental concerns, and promote unified products, damaging national cultural identities.

Arbitrage: exploitation of price and cost differential between markets. Ghemawat develops this concept further in his 2003 article "The Forgotten Strategy," in which he conceptualizes each dimension of distance as a potential source of arbitrage opportunities based on differences between markets.

Asian Currency Crisis: a financial crisis that occurred in a number of Asian countries in 1997. It manifested in a lack of foreign currency to maintain the national currency exchange rates, resulting in a drop of national currency value and a sharp increase in the debt-to-GDP ratios in the affected countries.

Brexit: a popular term, coined by combining words "Britain" and "exit," referring to the United Kingdom's departure from the European

Union (EU). In a 2016 referendum, 51.9% of participating voters voted to leave the EU, and the process is due to complete in 2019.

Commonwealth: The Commonwealth of Nations is an intergovernmental organization uniting 52 countries, mostly former parts of the British Empire that have gained independence.

Country Portfolio Analysis: an analysis technique used to assess potential target countries in which a company might compete. It mostly focuses on potential sales in each target market by looking at national GDP, levels of consumer wealth and its inhabitants' propensity to consume.

Country Premium (Country Risk Premium): additional risk that is associated with investing in a foreign country in comparison to domestic economy.

Cross-border management: see International business.

DHL: German postal service and world's largest logistics company, specializing in sea and air mail delivery. It's trade name is Deutsche Post DHL Group.

DHL Global Connectedness Index: a detailed analysis of the state of globalization around the world, measured by cross-border flows of trade, capital, information and people. It is published annually by DHL.

Dot-com Bubble: an overestimation of the value of Internet-based businesses that occurred in 1997-2001, leading venture capitalists to invest in such companies indiscriminately. Most of the new companies failed to deliver any profit, investors lost their money, and the market shrank rapidly.

Econometrics: application of statistical methods to explore phenomena in spheres of economics and business.

Economies of experience: The concept of economies of experience refers to the fact that productivity tends to increase with learning because, for example, the more a specific task is repeated, the quicker individuals or teams are likely to complete it.

Economies of scale: The relative gain in output or cost saving resulting from the greater efficiency of large-scale processes.

Entry strategy: a method of delivering and distributing goods and services in a new (including foreign) market chosen by a firm.

European Union: a political and economic union of countries located in Europe that currently counts 28 member states. The union has developed a common market and a number of standardized laws and regulations that apply to all member states.

Foreign Direct Investment (FDI): investment made by a firm or individual from one country into a business in another country either by establishing operations or buying existent assets.

Global Financial Crisis: the international banking crisis that started with a crisis in subprime mortgage market in USA in 2007 and escalated into the global financial market in 2008. It manifested in many banks going bankrupt or being bailed out by the state, global market indexes dropping, and a general economic recession.

Globalization: the increase in integration of local economies into a single global economy by means that include free trade and the free flow of capital and labor.

Globaloney: the tendency to overestimate the effects of globalization, such as the ratio of international trade to gross domestic product. The term was coined by combining the words "globalization" and "baloney."

Glocalization: a term, coined by combining the terms "globalization" and "localization," denoting the phenomenon of multinational companies designing their products or services to be distributed globally, but also to accommodate local requirements.

International business: trades and transactions that are performed internationally, including export and import of goods and services. International business is often referred to as cross-border management.

Knowledge spillover: a phenomenon that occurs when an exchange of information and ideas between individuals, units, or firms inadvertently stimulates innovation by the party that has not carried the costs of research and development for the initial idea that is being shared.

Knowledge transfer: the organized process through which written or tacit knowledge from one company, unit, team, or individual is transferred to another.

The Law of Distance: the observed phenomenon that international interactions are inhibited by cultural, administrative, geographic, and economic distance between countries.

The Law of Semiglobalization: the general rule that modern international interactions are significant, but yield to domestic interactions in intensity.

Mergers and Acquisitions (M&A): an umbrella term used to denote various ways for companies to consolidate assets, for example through one company becoming a part of another and ceasing to exist as a separate entity (merger) or through one company buying a majority stake in another (acquisition).

Multinational Enterprise (MNE): a company that controls production and/or distribution of goods or services in countries other than its home country. It can be also referred to as a multinational, multinational corporation, transnational enterprise or corporation, and international enterprise or corporation.

Net Present Value (NPV): the difference between the present value of cash inflows generated by business and the present value of cash outflows that are used to finance it. It is used to assess profitability of potential investment projects.

Own [foreign] operations: firm-owned production or distribution outlets in a foreign country.

Protectionism: measures, including tariffs and restrictions on imports and foreign direct investors, taken by national governments to protect local economies from foreign competition.

Regionalization: the phenomenon in which international trade intensifies within a group of countries that are located close to each other, i.e. within a region, whereas trade with countries outside the region may remain limited.

Satellite Television Asian Region (STAR): an Asian television service launched by Australian-American media mogul Rupert Murdoch in 1991. The initial strategy was to broadcast popular

English-language programming to Asian audience with little or no investment in new local programs. During the '90s, Star TV reportedly lost hundreds of millions of dollars every year and generated no profit until 2002.

Semiglobalization: a situation in which international trade intensifies and links between national markets are very strong, but the barriers between them are significant and cannot be neglected.

Theory of Multinational Enterprise: a theory formulated by Peter Buckley and Mark Casson, used to explain the existence of multinational enterprise as well as the processes of firms' international expansion. It emphasizes market imperfections and firms' inability to find markets for their product or services in their countries as the main underlying causes of internationalization.

Thinkers50: a global ranking of management thinkers, published biannually since 2001. The aim of the ranking is to identify, rank, and share leading management concepts, providing access to useful ideas.

Tricon Restaurant International: the international operating arm of Tricon Global Restaurant, Inc, the owner of fast-food brands such as Pizza Hut, Taco Bell, and KFC, which was spun off from PepsiCo in 1997. Tricon changed its corporate name in 2002 and it is now known as Yum! Brands, Inc.

PEOPLE MENTIONED IN THE TEXT

Pol Antràs (b. 1975) is Robert G. Ory Professor of Economics at Harvard University. Outside of his academic career, he has served as Director of the International Trade and Organization (ITO) Working Group at the National Bureau of Economic Research (NBER).

Ilgaz Arikan (b. 1971) is Assistant Professor of Management and Informational Systems at Kent State University. His chief academic interest is in firms' choices between initial public offerings, mergers, and acquisitions.

Christian Geisler Asmussen is Professor MSO at the Department of Strategic Management and Globalization at Copenhagen Business School. His primary research interests lie in the area of international diversification and MNE strategies.

Christopher A. Bartlett (b. 1943) is an Emeritus Professor at Harvard Business School, best known for his work in the sphere of International Management. In co-authorship with Sumantra Ghoshal, he wrote a number of works describing how firms manage their operations across national borders.

Peter Jennings Buckley (b. 1949) is Professor of International Business at Leeds University Business School. He co-authored the internalization theory of multinational enterprise with Mark Casson.

Joanna Tochman Campbell is an Assistant Professor of Management at the Carl H. Lindner College of Business at the University of Cincinnati. She studies the effect of executive characteristics on organizational outcomes, including in international settings.

Mark Casson (b. 1945) is Professor of Economics at the University of Reading. He co-authored the internalization theory of multinational enterprise with Peter J. Buckley.

Rian Drogendijk is Associate Professor of International Management at Uppsala University. Her main area of expertise is knowledge transfer and communication in multinational enterprises.

Lorraine Eden is Professor of Management at Texas A&M University. She is a renowned expert on transfer pricing between the subunits of multinational enterprises.

Jeffrey Alexander Frankel (b. 1952) is the James W. Harpel Professor of Capital Formation and Growth at the Kennedy School of Government, Harvard University. He is a macroeconomist studying international trade.

Thomas L. Friedman (b. 1953) is an American journalist and columnist for The New York Times. He has won the Pulitzer Prize—one of the most important journalism awards in the world—three times in 1983, 1988, and 2002 for his work on international affairs.

Sumantra Ghoshal (1948–2004) was Professor of Strategic and International Management at the London Business School. His work was dedicated to uncovering the different ways in which multinational enterprises manage their operations across national borders.

Stuart L. Hart is an academic studying the implications of environment for business strategy and a Fortune 100 consultant. He founded a non-profit organization called "Enterprise for a Sustainable World" to help businesses transition to sustainability.

Anne-Wil Harzing is a professor of International Management at Middlesex University London whose research focuses on expatriate and cross-cultural management.

John F. Helliwell (b.1937) is a Canadian economist, and editor of the annual World Happiness Report published by the United Nations. Helliwell studies international links between economies as well as the issues of happiness and wellbeing across the world.

Geert Hofstede (b.1928) is a Dutch social psychologist who pioneered cross-cultural organizational studies. His most famous work, *Culture's Consequences*, unveils the different dimensions on which organizational cultures differ across countries.

John Jullens is a management consultant specializing in the area of Global Strategy. He is a partner at Strategy&, leading the Engineered Products & Services division in China.

Art Kleiner is editor-in-chief of *strategy+business*, an influential American magazine for management practitioners focusing on issues of corporate strategy.

Bruce Kogut (b. 1953) is Professor of Leadership and Ethics Director of the Columbia Business School at Columbia University. He is an organizational theorist known particularly for his seminal works on knowledge transfer. Together with Harbir Singh, he described the effect of national cultures on entry modes.

Pascal Lamy (b. 1947) is a political consultant and businessman. He was the European Commissioner for Trade in 1999-2004, and headed the World Trade Organization as its Director-General from 2005 to 2013.

Dovev Lavie is Professor of Management at the Department of Management and Technology of Bocconi University (Milan, Italy), whose research interests lie in the area of resource-based theory.

Oscar Martín Martín is Associate Professor at the Public University of Navarre (Pamplona, Spain). His research interests center around multinational enterprises and their performance.

Stewart R. Miller is Professor of Management at the University of Texas at San Antonio, doing research in internationalization and emerging markets.

Lilach Nachum is Professor of International Business at the Zicklin School of Business at Baruch College (New York). Her work centers on multinational companies and the liability of foreignness.

Michael Porter (b.1947) is one of the most cited scholars in business and economics. Across his career, he has studied a number of issues pertaining to strategic management and founded a consulting company, The Monitor Group, which is now a part of Deloitte.

Coimbatore Krishnarao Prahalad (1941–2010) was the Paul and Ruth McCracken Distinguished University Professor of Corporate Strategy at the Stephen M. Ross School of Business, University of Michigan. He studied the business models of organizations and how they can improve public welfare.

Andrew K. Rose (b. 1959) is the B.T. Rocca Professor of Economic Analysis and Policy at Haas School of Business, University of California, Berkeley. He is a macroeconomist studying international trade and currency unions.

Alan M. Rugman (1945-2014) was a leading scholar in the field of international business. He actively participated in the debate surrounding Thomas Friedman's book *The World is Flat,* suggesting that multinational companies mostly operate regionally rather than globally.

Robert Salomon is Associate Professor of International Management and a Faculty Scholar at the NYU Stern School of Business. Among his research interests are foreign entry, location decisions, and cross-border knowledge transfer.

Margaret Schomaker is Professor at Université Laval (Quebec, Canada). Her research interests include mergers and acquisitions, international expansion, and subsidiaries' identities.

Beheruz Nariman Sethna (b. 1948) has served as the President of the University of West Georgia (USA) from 1994 to 2013. He has also published a number of academic articles on higher education, computerization, and user-generated content.

Scott Shane is Professor of Entrepreneurial Studies and Economics at Case Western Reserve University. His research focuses on new firm formation and economic development in different countries.

Oded Shenkar (b. 1951) is Professor of Management and Human Resources at Ohio State University. He studies management systems in different countries and advises a number of multinational enterprises and policy makers.

Harbir Singh is Professor of Management and Co-Director of Mack Institute for Innovation Management at the Wharton School, University of Pennsylvania. His research focuses on international business, particularly on international integration and alliances. Together with Bruce Kogut, he described the effect of national cultures on entry modes.

Donald Trump (b. 1946) is the 45th President of the United States, a businessman, and a former television show host. His election campaign relied on promises of protectionist policies.

Eric W. K. Tsang is Professor of Strategy and International Management at the University of Texas at Dallas. He researches organizational learning, including that carried out at multinationals.

Alain Verbeke is Professor of International Business Strategy at the Haskayne School of Business, University of Calgary. He studies strategies of multinational enterprises, mainly pertaining to the locus of their operations, e.g. regional or global.

Zheying Wu is a Researcher at the Department of Management at School of Economics and Management, Tilburg University (The Netherlands). Her research focuses on international business, particularly on entry strategies.

Paul Sau Leung Yip is an Associate Professor in Economics at Nanyang Technological University (Singapore). His research interests lie in the sphere of international monetary economics.

Srilata Zaheer is Elmer L. Andersen Chair in Global Corporate Social Responsibility and Dean at the Carlson School of Management, at the University of Minnesota. Her research focus is on international business and firms' location choices.

WORKS CITED

WORKS CITED

Albrow, Martin, and Elizabeth King, eds. *Globalization, Knowledge and Society.* London: Sage, 1990.

Anonymous, "About Pankaj Ghemawat." *Ghemawat.com*. Accessed November 13, 2017. https://www.ghemawat.com/about.

Anonymous, "DHL Global Connectedness Index 2016." *DHL*. Accessed November 13, 2017. http://www.dhl.com/en/about_us/logistics_insights/studies_research/global_connectedness_index/global_connectedness_index.html#.VFff5MkpXuM.

Anonymous, "Guru: Pankaj Ghemawat." *The Economist*. August 7, 2009. http://www.economist.com/node/14201826

Anonymous, "Pankaj Ghemawat." *The Economist*, August 7, 2009. Accessed November 13, 2017. http://www.economist.com/node/14201826.

Anonymous, "The Case Against Globaloney." *The Economist,* April 20, 2011. Accessed 26 October 2017. http://www.economist.com/node/18584204.

Anonymous, "The retreat of the global company." *The Economist*, January 28, 2017. Accessed November 13, 2017. https://www.economist.com/news/briefing/21715653-biggest-business-idea-past-three-decades-deep-trouble-retreat-global.

Arikan, Ilgaz, and Oded Shenkar. "National animosity and cross-border alliances." *Academy of Management Journal* 56 (2013): 1516-1544. doi: 10.5465/amj.2011.0210.

Buckley, Peter J., and Mark Casson. *The Future of the Multinational Enterprise.* London: Macmillan, 1976.

Campbell, Joanna Tochman, Lorraine Eden, and Stewart R. Miller. "Multinationals and corporate social responsibility in host countries: Does distance matter?" *Journal of International Business Studies* 43 (2012): 84-106. doi: 10.1057/jibs.2011.45.

Frankel, Jeffrey. A. "Measuring international capital mobility: a review." *American Economic Review* 82 (1992): 197-202.

Frankel, Jeffrey, and Andrew Rose. "An Estimate of the Effects of Common Currencies on Trade and Income." *The Quarterly Journal of Economics* 117 (2002): 437-466. doi: 10.1162/003355302753650292.

Friedman, Thomas. *The World Is Flat: The Globalized World in the Twenty-First Century.* London: Penguin, 2007.

Ghemawat, Pankaj. "Distance Still Matters: The Hard Reality of Global Expansion." *Harvard Business Review,* September, 2001, 138-139.

- "Globalization in the Age of Trump." *Harvard Business Review,* July-August, 2017, 112-123.

- "Globalization: The Strategy of Differences." *Working Knowledge*, October 15, 2007. Accessed November 13, 2017. http://hbswk.hbs.edu/item/3773.html.

- "Managing Differences: The Central Challenge of Global Strategy." *Harvard Business Review*, March, 2007, 58-68.

- "People Are Angry About Globalization. Here's What to Do About It." *Harvard Business Review Digital Articles* (November 2016). Accessed October 26, 2017. https://hbr.org/2016/11/people-are-angry-about-globalization-heres-what-to-do-about-it.

- "Semiglobalization and International Business Strategy." *Journal of International Business Studies* 34 (2003): 138-152. doi: 10.1057/palgrave. jibs.8400013.

- "The Forgotten Strategy." *Harvard Business Review,* November, 2003, 76-84.

- *The Laws of Globalization and Business Applications.* Cambridge: Cambridge University Press, 2016.

- *World 3.0: Global Prosperity and How to Achieve It.* Boston, MA, US: Harvard Business School Press, 2011.

Ghemawat, Pankaj, and Steven A. Altman. "DHL Global Connectedness Index 2012." *DHL*. Accessed November 13, 2017. http://www.dhl.com/content/dam/flash/g0/gci_2012/download/dhl_gci_2012_complete_study.pdf.

Ghoshal, Sumantra. "Global strategy: An organizing framework." *Strategic management journal* 8 (1987): 425-440.

Giudici, Alessandro, and Patrick Reinmoeller. "Dynamic capabilities in the dock: A case of reification?" *Strategic Organization* 10 (2012): 436-449, doi: 10.1177/1476127012457977.

Harzing, Anne-Wil, "The Role of Culture in Entry-Mode Studies: From Neglect to Myopia?" In *Managing Multinationals in a Knowledge Economy: Economics, Culture, and Human Resources*, edited by Joseph L. C. Cheng and Michael A. Hitt, 75– 127. Bingley: Emerald Group Publishing Limited, 2003.

Helliwell, John F. *How Much Do National Borders Matter?* Washington, DC: Brookings Institution Press, 1998.

Hindle, Tim. *The Economist's Guide to Management Gurus and Ideas.* London: Economist Books, 2012.

Hofstede, Geert. *Culture's Consequences.* New York: Sage, 1980.

Jullens, John. "The Flat World Debate Revisited." *strategy+business*, May 6, 2013. Accessed 13 November, 2017. http://www.strategy-business.com/article/00190?gko=403fb.

- "Friedman versus Ghemawat - How Flat is the World Really?" *John Jullens Global Perspectives* (January, 2013). Accessed November 29, 2017. http://www.johnjullens.com/show.php?NewsId=67.

Keller, Wolfgang. "Geographic Localization of International Technology Diffusion." Working Paper No. 750, *National Bureau of Economic Research*, 2000.

Kogut, Bruce, and Harbir Singh. "The effect of national culture on the choice of entry mode." *Journal of International Business Studies* 19 (1988): 411-432. doi: 10.1057/palgrave.jibs.8490394.

Kostova, Tatiana, Phillip C. Nell, and Anne K. Hoenen. "Understanding Agency Problems in Headquarters-Subsidiary Relationships in Multinational Corporations: A Contextualized Model." *Journal of Management* 5 (2016): 1-27. doi: 10.1177/0149206316648383.

Lagace, Martha. "Businesses Beware: The World Is Not Flat." *Working Knowledge*, October 15, 2007. Accessed November 13, 2017. http://hbswk.hbs.edu/item/5719.html.

Lavie, Dovev, and Stewart R. Miller. "Alliance Portfolio Internationalization and Firm Performance." *Organization Science* 19 (2008): 623-646. doi: 10.1287/orsc.1070.0341.

Maddison, Angus. *Monitoring the World Economy: 1820–1992.* Development Centre of the Organization for Economic Cooperation and Development: Paris, 1995.

Martín, Oscar Martín, and Rian Drogendijk. "Country Distance (COD): Development and Validation of a New Objective Measure." *Journal of Small Business Management* 52 (2014): 102-125. doi: 10.1111/jsbm.12035.

Nachum, Lilach, and Srilata Zaheer. "The Persistence of Distance? The Impact of Technology on MNE Motivations for Foreign Investment." *Strategic Management Journal* 26 (2005): 747-768. doi: 10.1002/smj.472.

Parker, Ceri. "The end of globalization? Davos disagrees." *World Economic Forum,* January 20, 2017. Accessed November 20, 2017. https://www.weforum.org/agenda/2017/01/the-end-of-globalization-davos-disagrees/.

Porter, Michael E. "The Competitive Advantage of Nations." *Harvard Business Review,* March-April, 1990, 73-93.

Prahalad, Coimbatore K., and Stuart L. Hart. "The Fortune at the Bottom of the Pyramid." *strategy+business* 26 (2002). Accessed 20 October 2017. https://www.strategy-business.com/article/11518?gko=9a4ba.

Rugman, Alan. *The End of Globalization*. Random House Business Books, 2012. Accessed November 25, 2017. https://www.penguin.co.uk/books/1046014/the-end-of-globalization/.

Salomon, Robert M. *Global Vision: How Companies Can Overcome the Pitfalls of Globalization*. New York: Palgrave Macmillan, 2016.

Salomon, Robert, and Zheying Wu. "Institutional distance and local isomorphism strategy." *Journal of International Business Studies* 43 (2012): 343-367. doi: 10.1057/jibs.2012.3.

Search term "Distance Still Matters." *Google Scholar.* Accessed October 20, 2017. https://scholar.google.com/scholar?hl=ru&as_sdt=0,5&q=distance+still+matters.

Search term "Distance Still Matters." *Web of Science*. Accessed October 20, 2017. https://apps.webofknowledge.com/full_record.do?product=WOS&search_mode=GeneralSearch&qid=3&SID=C6yvoy6nVHcouLE5d7K&page=1&doc=1&cacheurlFromRightClick=no.

Search term "Globalization." *Google NGram*. Accessed October 20, 2017. https://books.google.com/ngrams/graph?content=globalization&year_start=1800&year_end=2.000&corpus=15&smoothing=3&share=&direct_url=t1%3B%2Cglobalization%3B%2CcO.

Sethna, Beheruz N. "Ghemawat v. Friedman: Is the World Flat?" *Decision Line* 39 (2008), 25-31.

Shane, Scott. "The effect of national culture on the choice between licensing and direct foreign investment." *Strategic Management Journal* 15 (1994): 627-642. doi: 10.1002/smj.4250150805.

Shenkar, Oded. "Cultural Distance Revisited: Towards a More Rigorous Conceptualization and Measurement of Cultural Differences." *Journal of International Business Studies* 32 (2001):519– 535. doi: 10.1057/palgrave. jibs.8490982.

- "The Case Against Globaloney." *The Economist,* April 20, 2011. Accessed 26 October 2017. http://www.economist.com/node/18584204.

Tsang, Eric W. L., and Paul S. L. Yip. "Economic Distance and the Survival of Foreign Direct Investments." *Academy of Management Journal* 50 (2007): 1156-1168. doi: 10.2307/20159917.

Verbeke, Alain, and Christian G. Asmussen. "Global, Local, or Regional? The Locus of MNE Strategies." *Journal of Management Studies* 53 (2016): 1051-1075. doi: 10.1111/joms.12190.

Zaheer, Srilata, Margaret Spring Schomaker, and Lilach Nachum. "Distance without Direction: Restoring Credibility to a Much-Loved Construct." *Journal of International Business Studies* 43 (2012):18– 27. doi: 10.1057/jibs.2011.43.

THE MACAT LIBRARY
BY DISCIPLINE

AFRICANA STUDIES

Chinua Achebe's *An Image of Africa: Racism in Conrad's Heart of Darkness*
W. E. B. Du Bois's *The Souls of Black Folk*
Zora Neale Huston's *Characteristics of Negro Expression*
Martin Luther King Jr's *Why We Can't Wait*
Toni Morrison's *Playing in the Dark: Whiteness in the American Literary Imagination*

ANTHROPOLOGY

Arjun Appadurai's *Modernity at Large: Cultural Dimensions of Globalisation*
Philippe Ariès's *Centuries of Childhood*
Franz Boas's *Race, Language and Culture*
Kim Chan & Renée Mauborgne's *Blue Ocean Strategy*
Jared Diamond's *Guns, Germs & Steel: the Fate of Human Societies*
Jared Diamond's *Collapse: How Societies Choose to Fail or Survive*
E. E. Evans-Pritchard's *Witchcraft, Oracles and Magic Among the Azande*
James Ferguson's *The Anti-Politics Machine*
Clifford Geertz's *The Interpretation of Cultures*
David Graeber's *Debt: the First 5000 Years*
Karen Ho's *Liquidated: An Ethnography of Wall Street*
Geert Hofstede's *Culture's Consequences: Comparing Values, Behaviors, Institutes and Organizations across Nations*
Claude Lévi-Strauss's *Structural Anthropology*
Jay Macleod's *Ain't No Makin' It: Aspirations and Attainment in a Low-Income Neighborhood*
Saba Mahmood's *The Politics of Piety: The Islamic Revival and the Feminist Subject*
Marcel Mauss's *The Gift*

BUSINESS

Jean Lave & Etienne Wenger's *Situated Learning*
Theodore Levitt's *Marketing Myopia*
Burton G. Malkiel's *A Random Walk Down Wall Street*
Douglas McGregor's *The Human Side of Enterprise*
Michael Porter's *Competitive Strategy: Creating and Sustaining Superior Performance*
John Kotter's *Leading Change*
C. K. Prahalad & Gary Hamel's *The Core Competence of the Corporation*

CRIMINOLOGY

Michelle Alexander's *The New Jim Crow: Mass Incarceration in the Age of Colorblindness*
Michael R. Gottfredson & Travis Hirschi's *A General Theory of Crime*
Richard Herrnstein & Charles A. Murray's *The Bell Curve: Intelligence and Class Structure in American Life*
Elizabeth Loftus's *Eyewitness Testimony*
Jay Macleod's *Ain't No Makin' It: Aspirations and Attainment in a Low-Income Neighborhood*
Philip Zimbardo's *The Lucifer Effect*

ECONOMICS

Janet Abu-Lughod's *Before European Hegemony*
Ha-Joon Chang's *Kicking Away the Ladder*
David Brion Davis's *The Problem of Slavery in the Age of Revolution*
Milton Friedman's *The Role of Monetary Policy*
Milton Friedman's *Capitalism and Freedom*
David Graeber's *Debt: the First 5000 Years*
Friedrich Hayek's *The Road to Serfdom*
Karen Ho's *Liquidated: An Ethnography of Wall Street*

John Maynard Keynes's *The General Theory of Employment, Interest and Money*
Charles P. Kindleberger's *Manias, Panics and Crashes*
Robert Lucas's *Why Doesn't Capital Flow from Rich to Poor Countries?*
Burton G. Malkiel's *A Random Walk Down Wall Street*
Thomas Robert Malthus's *An Essay on the Principle of Population*
Karl Marx's *Capital*
Thomas Piketty's *Capital in the Twenty-First Century*
Amartya Sen's *Development as Freedom*
Adam Smith's *The Wealth of Nations*
Nassim Nicholas Taleb's *The Black Swan: The Impact of the Highly Improbable*
Amos Tversky's & Daniel Kahneman's *Judgment under Uncertainty: Heuristics and Biases*
Mahbub Ul Haq's *Reflections on Human Development*
Max Weber's *The Protestant Ethic and the Spirit of Capitalism*

FEMINISM AND GENDER STUDIES

Judith Butler's *Gender Trouble*
Simone De Beauvoir's *The Second Sex*
Michel Foucault's *History of Sexuality*
Betty Friedan's *The Feminine Mystique*
Saba Mahmood's *The Politics of Piety: The Islamic Revival and the Feminist Subject*
Joan Wallach Scott's *Gender and the Politics of History*
Mary Wollstonecraft's *A Vindication of the Rights of Woman*
Virginia Woolf's *A Room of One's Own*

GEOGRAPHY

The Brundtland Report's *Our Common Future*
Rachel Carson's *Silent Spring*
Charles Darwin's *On the Origin of Species*
James Ferguson's *The Anti-Politics Machine*
Jane Jacobs's *The Death and Life of Great American Cities*
James Lovelock's *Gaia: A New Look at Life on Earth*
Amartya Sen's *Development as Freedom*
Mathis Wackernagel & William Rees's *Our Ecological Footprint*

HISTORY

Janet Abu-Lughod's *Before European Hegemony*
Benedict Anderson's *Imagined Communities*
Bernard Bailyn's *The Ideological Origins of the American Revolution*
Hanna Batatu's *The Old Social Classes And The Revolutionary Movements Of Iraq*
Christopher Browning's *Ordinary Men: Reserve Police Batallion 101 and the Final Solution in Poland*
Edmund Burke's *Reflections on the Revolution in France*
William Cronon's *Nature's Metropolis: Chicago And The Great West*
Alfred W. Crosby's *The Columbian Exchange*
Hamid Dabashi's *Iran: A People Interrupted*
David Brion Davis's *The Problem of Slavery in the Age of Revolution*
Nathalie Zemon Davis's *The Return of Martin Guerre*
Jared Diamond's *Guns, Germs & Steel: the Fate of Human Societies*
Frank Dikotter's *Mao's Great Famine*
John W Dower's *War Without Mercy: Race And Power In The Pacific War*
W. E. B. Du Bois's *The Souls of Black Folk*
Richard J. Evans's *In Defence of History*
Lucien Febvre's *The Problem of Unbelief in the 16th Century*
Sheila Fitzpatrick's *Everyday Stalinism*

Eric Foner's *Reconstruction: America's Unfinished Revolution, 1863-1877*
Michel Foucault's *Discipline and Punish*
Michel Foucault's *History of Sexuality*
Francis Fukuyama's *The End of History and the Last Man*
John Lewis Gaddis's *We Now Know: Rethinking Cold War History*
Ernest Gellner's *Nations and Nationalism*
Eugene Genovese's *Roll, Jordan, Roll: The World the Slaves Made*
Carlo Ginzburg's *The Night Battles*
Daniel Goldhagen's *Hitler's Willing Executioners*
Jack Goldstone's *Revolution and Rebellion in the Early Modern World*
Antonio Gramsci's *The Prison Notebooks*
Alexander Hamilton, John Jay & James Madison's *The Federalist Papers*
Christopher Hill's *The World Turned Upside Down*
Carole Hillenbrand's *The Crusades: Islamic Perspectives*
Thomas Hobbes's *Leviathan*
Eric Hobsbawm's *The Age Of Revolution*
John A. Hobson's *Imperialism: A Study*
Albert Hourani's *History of the Arab Peoples*
Samuel P. Huntington's *The Clash of Civilizations and the Remaking of World Order*
C. L. R. James's *The Black Jacobins*
Tony Judt's *Postwar: A History of Europe Since 1945*
Ernst Kantorowicz's *The King's Two Bodies: A Study in Medieval Political Theology*
Paul Kennedy's *The Rise and Fall of the Great Powers*
Ian Kershaw's *The "Hitler Myth": Image and Reality in the Third Reich*
John Maynard Keynes's *The General Theory of Employment, Interest and Money*
Charles P. Kindleberger's *Manias, Panics and Crashes*
Martin Luther King Jr's *Why We Can't Wait*
Henry Kissinger's *World Order: Reflections on the Character of Nations and the Course of History*
Thomas Kuhn's *The Structure of Scientific Revolutions*
Georges Lefebvre's *The Coming of the French Revolution*
John Locke's *Two Treatises of Government*
Niccolò Machiavelli's *The Prince*
Thomas Robert Malthus's *An Essay on the Principle of Population*
Mahmood Mamdani's *Citizen and Subject: Contemporary Africa And The Legacy Of Late Colonialism*
Karl Marx's *Capital*
Stanley Milgram's *Obedience to Authority*
John Stuart Mill's *On Liberty*
Thomas Paine's *Common Sense*
Thomas Paine's *Rights of Man*
Geoffrey Parker's *Global Crisis: War, Climate Change and Catastrophe in the Seventeenth Century*
Jonathan Riley-Smith's *The First Crusade and the Idea of Crusading*
Jean-Jacques Rousseau's *The Social Contract*
Joan Wallach Scott's *Gender and the Politics of History*
Theda Skocpol's *States and Social Revolutions*
Adam Smith's *The Wealth of Nations*
Timothy Snyder's *Bloodlands: Europe Between Hitler and Stalin*
Sun Tzu's *The Art of War*
Keith Thomas's *Religion and the Decline of Magic*
Thucydides's *The History of the Peloponnesian War*
Frederick Jackson Turner's *The Significance of the Frontier in American History*
Odd Arne Westad's *The Global Cold War: Third World Interventions And The Making Of Our Times*

LITERATURE

Chinua Achebe's *An Image of Africa: Racism in Conrad's Heart of Darkness*
Roland Barthes's *Mythologies*
Homi K. Bhabha's *The Location of Culture*
Judith Butler's *Gender Trouble*
Simone De Beauvoir's *The Second Sex*
Ferdinand De Saussure's *Course in General Linguistics*
T. S. Eliot's *The Sacred Wood: Essays on Poetry and Criticism*
Zora Neale Huston's *Characteristics of Negro Expression*
Toni Morrison's *Playing in the Dark: Whiteness in the American Literary Imagination*
Edward Said's *Orientalism*
Gayatri Chakravorty Spivak's *Can the Subaltern Speak?*
Mary Wollstonecraft's *A Vindication of the Rights of Women*
Virginia Woolf's *A Room of One's Own*

PHILOSOPHY

Elizabeth Anscombe's *Modern Moral Philosophy*
Hannah Arendt's *The Human Condition*
Aristotle's *Metaphysics*
Aristotle's *Nicomachean Ethics*
Edmund Gettier's *Is Justified True Belief Knowledge?*
Georg Wilhelm Friedrich Hegel's *Phenomenology of Spirit*
David Hume's *Dialogues Concerning Natural Religion*
David Hume's *The Enquiry for Human Understanding*
Immanuel Kant's *Religion within the Boundaries of Mere Reason*
Immanuel Kant's *Critique of Pure Reason*
Søren Kierkegaard's *The Sickness Unto Death*
Søren Kierkegaard's *Fear and Trembling*
C. S. Lewis's *The Abolition of Man*
Alasdair MacIntyre's *After Virtue*
Marcus Aurelius's *Meditations*
Friedrich Nietzsche's *On the Genealogy of Morality*
Friedrich Nietzsche's *Beyond Good and Evil*
Plato's *Republic*
Plato's *Symposium*
Jean-Jacques Rousseau's *The Social Contract*
Gilbert Ryle's *The Concept of Mind*
Baruch Spinoza's *Ethics*
Sun Tzu's *The Art of War*
Ludwig Wittgenstein's *Philosophical Investigations*

POLITICS

Benedict Anderson's *Imagined Communities*
Aristotle's *Politics*
Bernard Bailyn's *The Ideological Origins of the American Revolution*
Edmund Burke's *Reflections on the Revolution in France*
John C. Calhoun's *A Disquisition on Government*
Ha-Joon Chang's *Kicking Away the Ladder*
Hamid Dabashi's *Iran: A People Interrupted*
Hamid Dabashi's *Theology of Discontent: The Ideological Foundation of the Islamic Revolution in Iran*
Robert Dahl's *Democracy and its Critics*
Robert Dahl's *Who Governs?*
David Brion Davis's *The Problem of Slavery in the Age of Revolution*

The Macat Library By Discipline

Alexis De Tocqueville's *Democracy in America*
James Ferguson's *The Anti-Politics Machine*
Frank Dikotter's *Mao's Great Famine*
Sheila Fitzpatrick's *Everyday Stalinism*
Eric Foner's *Reconstruction: America's Unfinished Revolution, 1863-1877*
Milton Friedman's *Capitalism and Freedom*
Francis Fukuyama's *The End of History and the Last Man*
John Lewis Gaddis's *We Now Know: Rethinking Cold War History*
Ernest Gellner's *Nations and Nationalism*
David Graeber's *Debt: the First 5000 Years*
Antonio Gramsci's *The Prison Notebooks*
Alexander Hamilton, John Jay & James Madison's *The Federalist Papers*
Friedrich Hayek's *The Road to Serfdom*
Christopher Hill's *The World Turned Upside Down*
Thomas Hobbes's *Leviathan*
John A. Hobson's *Imperialism: A Study*
Samuel P. Huntington's *The Clash of Civilizations and the Remaking of World Order*
Tony Judt's *Postwar: A History of Europe Since 1945*
David C. Kang's *China Rising: Peace, Power and Order in East Asia*
Paul Kennedy's *The Rise and Fall of Great Powers*
Robert Keohane's *After Hegemony*
Martin Luther King Jr.'s *Why We Can't Wait*
Henry Kissinger's *World Order: Reflections on the Character of Nations and the Course of History*
John Locke's *Two Treatises of Government*
Niccolò Machiavelli's *The Prince*
Thomas Robert Malthus's *An Essay on the Principle of Population*
Mahmood Mamdani's *Citizen and Subject: Contemporary Africa And The Legacy Of Late Colonialism*
Karl Marx's *Capital*
John Stuart Mill's *On Liberty*
John Stuart Mill's *Utilitarianism*
Hans Morgenthau's *Politics Among Nations*
Thomas Paine's *Common Sense*
Thomas Paine's *Rights of Man*
Thomas Piketty's *Capital in the Twenty-First Century*
Robert D. Putman's *Bowling Alone*
John Rawls's *Theory of Justice*
Jean-Jacques Rousseau's *The Social Contract*
Theda Skocpol's *States and Social Revolutions*
Adam Smith's *The Wealth of Nations*
Sun Tzu's *The Art of War*
Henry David Thoreau's *Civil Disobedience*
Thucydides's *The History of the Peloponnesian War*
Kenneth Waltz's *Theory of International Politics*
Max Weber's *Politics as a Vocation*
Odd Arne Westad's *The Global Cold War: Third World Interventions And The Making Of Our Times*

POSTCOLONIAL STUDIES

Roland Barthes's *Mythologies*
Frantz Fanon's *Black Skin, White Masks*
Homi K. Bhabha's *The Location of Culture*
Gustavo Gutiérrez's *A Theology of Liberation*
Edward Said's *Orientalism*
Gayatri Chakravorty Spivak's *Can the Subaltern Speak?*

PSYCHOLOGY

Gordon Allport's *The Nature of Prejudice*
Alan Baddeley & Graham Hitch's *Aggression: A Social Learning Analysis*
Albert Bandura's *Aggression: A Social Learning Analysis*
Leon Festinger's *A Theory of Cognitive Dissonance*
Sigmund Freud's *The Interpretation of Dreams*
Betty Friedan's *The Feminine Mystique*
Michael R. Gottfredson & Travis Hirschi's *A General Theory of Crime*
Eric Hoffer's *The True Believer: Thoughts on the Nature of Mass Movements*
William James's *Principles of Psychology*
Elizabeth Loftus's *Eyewitness Testimony*
A. H. Maslow's *A Theory of Human Motivation*
Stanley Milgram's *Obedience to Authority*
Steven Pinker's *The Better Angels of Our Nature*
Oliver Sacks's *The Man Who Mistook His Wife For a Hat*
Richard Thaler & Cass Sunstein's *Nudge: Improving Decisions About Health, Wealth and Happiness*
Amos Tversky's *Judgment under Uncertainty: Heuristics and Biases*
Philip Zimbardo's *The Lucifer Effect*

SCIENCE

Rachel Carson's *Silent Spring*
William Cronon's *Nature's Metropolis: Chicago And The Great West*
Alfred W. Crosby's *The Columbian Exchange*
Charles Darwin's *On the Origin of Species*
Richard Dawkin's *The Selfish Gene*
Thomas Kuhn's *The Structure of Scientific Revolutions*
Geoffrey Parker's *Global Crisis: War, Climate Change and Catastrophe in the Seventeenth Century*
Mathis Wackernagel & William Rees's *Our Ecological Footprint*

SOCIOLOGY

Michelle Alexander's *The New Jim Crow: Mass Incarceration in the Age of Colorblindness*
Gordon Allport's *The Nature of Prejudice*
Albert Bandura's *Aggression: A Social Learning Analysis*
Hanna Batatu's *The Old Social Classes And The Revolutionary Movements Of Iraq*
Ha-Joon Chang's *Kicking Away the Ladder*
W. E. B. Du Bois's *The Souls of Black Folk*
Émile Durkheim's *On Suicide*
Frantz Fanon's *Black Skin, White Masks*
Frantz Fanon's *The Wretched of the Earth*
Eric Foner's *Reconstruction: America's Unfinished Revolution, 1863-1877*
Eugene Genovese's *Roll, Jordan, Roll: The World the Slaves Made*
Jack Goldstone's *Revolution and Rebellion in the Early Modern World*
Antonio Gramsci's *The Prison Notebooks*
Richard Herrnstein & Charles A Murray's *The Bell Curve: Intelligence and Class Structure in American Life*
Eric Hoffer's *The True Believer: Thoughts on the Nature of Mass Movements*
Jane Jacobs's *The Death and Life of Great American Cities*
Robert Lucas's *Why Doesn't Capital Flow from Rich to Poor Countries?*
Jay Macleod's *Ain't No Makin' It: Aspirations and Attainment in a Low Income Neighborhood*
Elaine May's *Homeward Bound: American Families in the Cold War Era*
Douglas McGregor's *The Human Side of Enterprise*
C. Wright Mills's *The Sociological Imagination*

Thomas Piketty's *Capital in the Twenty-First Century*
Robert D. Putman's *Bowling Alone*
David Riesman's *The Lonely Crowd: A Study of the Changing American Character*
Edward Said's *Orientalism*
Joan Wallach Scott's *Gender and the Politics of History*
Theda Skocpol's *States and Social Revolutions*
Max Weber's *The Protestant Ethic and the Spirit of Capitalism*

THEOLOGY

Augustine's *Confessions*
Benedict's *Rule of St Benedict*
Gustavo Gutiérrez's *A Theology of Liberation*
Carole Hillenbrand's *The Crusades: Islamic Perspectives*
David Hume's *Dialogues Concerning Natural Religion*
Immanuel Kant's *Religion within the Boundaries of Mere Reason*
Ernst Kantorowicz's *The King's Two Bodies: A Study in Medieval Political Theology*
Søren Kierkegaard's *The Sickness Unto Death*
C. S. Lewis's *The Abolition of Man*
Saba Mahmood's *The Politics of Piety: The Islamic Revival and the Feminist Subject*
Baruch Spinoza's *Ethics*
Keith Thomas's *Religion and the Decline of Magic*

Macat Disciplines

Access the greatest ideas and thinkers across entire disciplines, including

Macat Pairs

*Analyse historical and modern issues
from opposite sides of an argument.
Pairs include:*

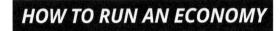

HOW TO RUN AN ECONOMY

John Maynard Keynes's
*The General Theory OF Employment,
Interest and Money*

Classical economics suggests that market economies are self-correcting in times of recession or depression, and tend toward full employment and output. But English economist John Maynard Keynes disagrees.

In his ground-breaking 1936 study *The General Theory*, Keynes argues that traditional economics has misunderstood the causes of unemployment. Employment is not determined by the price of labor; it is directly linked to demand. Keynes believes market economies are by nature unstable, and so require government intervention. Spurred on by the social catastrophe of the Great Depression of the 1930s, he sets out to revolutionize the way the world thinks

Milton Friedman's
The Role of Monetary Policy

Friedman's 1968 paper changed the course of economic theory. In just 17 pages, he demolished existing theory and outlined an effective alternate monetary policy designed to secure 'high employment, stable prices and rapid growth.'

Friedman demonstrated that monetary policy plays a vital role in broader economic stability and argued that economists got their monetary policy wrong in the 1950s and 1960s by misunderstanding the relationship between inflation and unemployment. Previous generations of economists had believed that governments could permanently decrease unemployment by permitting inflation—and vice versa. Friedman's most original contribution was to show that this supposed trade-off is an illusion that only works in the short term.

Macat analyses are available from all good bookshops and libraries.

Access hundreds of analyses through one, multimedia tool.
Join free for one month **library.macat.com**

Macat Disciplines

Access the greatest ideas and thinkers across entire disciplines, including

THE FUTURE OF DEMOCRACY

Robert A. Dahl's, *Democracy and Its Critics*
Robert A. Dahl's, *Who Governs?*
Alexis De Toqueville's, *Democracy in America*
Niccolò Machiavelli's, *The Prince*
John Stuart Mill's, *On Liberty*
Robert D. Putnam's, *Bowling Alone*
Jean-Jacques Rousseau's, *The Social Contract*
Henry David Thoreau's, *Civil Disobedience*

Macat analyses are available from all good bookshops and libraries.

Access hundreds of analyses through one, multimedia tool.
Join free for one month **library.macat.com**

Macat Disciplines

Access the greatest ideas and thinkers across entire disciplines, including

Macat Pairs

Analyse historical and modern issues from opposite sides of an argument. Pairs include:

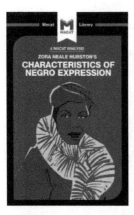

Macat Pairs

Analyse historical and modern issues from opposite sides of an argument. Pairs include:

ARE WE FUNDAMENTALLY GOOD - OR BAD?

Steven Pinker's
The Better Angels of Our Nature

Stephen Pinker's gloriously optimistic 2011 book argues that, despite humanity's biological tendency toward violence, we are, in fact, less violent today than ever before. To prove his case, Pinker lays out pages of detailed statistical evidence. For him, much of the credit for the decline goes to the eighteenth-century Enlightenment movement, whose ideas of liberty, tolerance, and respect for the value of human life filtered down through society and affected how people thought. That psychological change led to behavioral change—and overall we became more peaceful. Critics countered that humanity could never overcome the biological urge toward violence; others argued that Pinker's statistics were flawed.

Philip Zimbardo's
The Lucifer Effect

Some psychologists believe those who commit cruelty are innately evil. Zimbardo disagrees. In *The Lucifer Effect*, he argues that sometimes good people do evil things simply because of the situations they find themselves in, citing many historical examples to illustrate his point. Zimbardo details his 1971 Stanford prison experiment, where ordinary volunteers playing guards in a mock prison rapidly became abusive. But he also describes the tortures committed by US army personnel in Iraq's Abu Ghraib prison in 2003—and how he himself testified in defence of one of those guards. committed by US army personnel in Iraq's Abu Ghraib prison in 2003—and how he himself testified in defence of one of those guards.

Macat Pairs

Analyse historical and modern issues from opposite sides of an argument. Pairs include: